YOUR
HEALTHY
JOURNEY

DISCOVERING YOUR BODY'S FULL POTENTIAL

FRED BISCI, PhD

www.anydoubtleaveitout.com

www.fredbisci4health.com

Disclaimer: The information in this book is about a healthy lifestyle program that the author has advocated from over 50 years of his experience and working with tens of thousands of people. This is not intended for diagnosis and treatment of individual disease. Please consult a qualified medical professional when necessary.

Printed in the United States of America

ISBN: 978-0-9822130-0-1

Library of Congress Cataloging-in-Publication Data
Bisci, Fred A., 1929-
Your Healthy Journey: Discovering Your Body's Full Potential
Fred A. Bisci
Third Edition
Bisci Lifestyle Books

Art direction and design:
Enrique Candioti: ecandioti@gmail.com
Editor: Jonathan Collins: jaicollins@gmail.com
Contact website: www.anydoubtleaveitout.com
Cover photography: Robert Russell & AVTG photography
Back cover photo of Fred Bisci: Cheryll A. Lynn
Back cover photography: Jakub Sopicki

Contact e-mail:
webmaster@fredbisci4health.com, rorydf@yahoo.com

Your Healthy Journey Experiences

Your Healthy Journey reflects Dr. Bisci fifty plus years of experience working with more than 35,000 patients in the areas of nutritional prevention of illness and healing. As a true pioneer, teacher, and practitioner, Dr. Bisci walks the walk. As an accomplished athlete, he gained first hand, true life experience of how to be the best one can be both physically and spiritually through lifestyle and nutrition. He is one of the earliest promoters of the body, mind, and spirit connection. As an educated and trained nutritionist, he has selected the principle of a dominant raw food lifestyle, proper food combining, and acceptance of divine order in our lives as a formula for health, recovery and longevity.

Dr. Bisci recognizes the nutritional jungle has created confusion in the minds of those seeking help to answers questions regarding their health problems. In fact, in his book, he outlines the ABC's of what to do for maximum results. He clearly points to the main steps to take in this direction. These are, Phase of Adaptation, i.e. time needed for the body to accept a new, healthy lifestyle, Phase of Recuperation from injuries caused by harming our bodies, Phase of Stabilization during which our bodies will balance to its most natural weight, and the Phase of Anabolism, the time during which our physical bodies will build itself to its natural best. The Eating Guidelines he is proposing, which is a two to three well composed meals per day, is something that one can follow for lifelong benefits. Your Healthy Journey is a guide for good nutrition, health, happiness, productivity, and ultimately longevity.

E.K. Schandl, B.A., M.S., Ph.D.

Dr Fred Bisci was the fulcrum point for me in crystallizing how to gain the most healing and life sustaining nutrition. Fred, born in 1929, is a New York City based, lifestyle, food scientist that specializes in nutrition through lifestyle change. He has been working with individuals with chronic disease for over five decades with considerable success. Many of his clients reach him after following the convention medicine approach. I have found that when you are open to his advice there is a recovery that takes place or improvement in the quality of an extension of a person's life well beyond what was considered possible. Although following a 100% raw food lifestyle is not necessary to achieve healing, Fred is a living testimony to how healthy one can be by following a scientifically developed 100% raw plant-based lifestyle which he has assiduously pursued for over 50 years.

He is as fit as the proverbial Australian mallee bull. Fred recognizes that every human being is unique and has different chemical and emotional needs around food and tailors the fundamental to his method and nutritional recommendations to suit each person. He has developed a modified transition approach, some of which includes meat and cooked food portions for those that find a 100% raw food plant-based lifestyle just too difficult first up. I have learned vital information from Dr Bisci which has transformed the way I think about nutrition. Some of it was brand new to me while some of it I was aware of and either already living or ignoring at my peril. Fred is a living wakeup call. The key benefits I gained from him were the overview he provided, the scientific thinking he applies and the fact that he has experimented on his own life and has successfully helped family, friends and clients that were terminally ill. He is the real deal!

John A Wood /Former CEO & Chairman /Fleetwood Corp./AU

It is an honor and a privilege to know Dr. Fred Bisci. When we encountered health challenges with our own children, we sought the advice and knowledge of Dr. Fred. He has directly helped us from the day our children were born. Dr. Fred has consistently put us on the right track. We also know him as a most exceptional friend. The reason for his amazing success is his gifted ability to look at the body's biochemistry and then meet the person on his or her own level. Dr. Fred's wealth of nutritional knowledge is complemented by a fine eye that looks directly into the heart and mind of the people he works with to help raise them up. He is a sound and trustworthy being, really a gift to humanity. Never forcing radical lifestyle changes and always suggesting. Dr. Fred gently leads a person to his or her personal needs because he knows that there is never one perfect way for everyone.

Also never in the history of our harvesting has anyone researched and scrutinized our E3Live (Aphanizomenon flos-aquae) as extensively as Dr. Fred Bisci. He would not recommend it until it was thoroughly tested. We respect him for his ethics. In keeping with his sincere spirituality, the essential message he delivers is always the same: Love and compassion along with a healthy lifestyle are all major parts of a successful and satisfying life. I could not agree more.

Tamera Campbell, CEO & Master Harvester, Klamath algae Products

Dr. Fred Bisci has a sensible, honest approach to how the body heals. Most importantly, he emanates a sparkling health of body, spirit and mind. Being with Dr. Fred is a healing experience in itself. That is because he walks his walk and practices what he preaches.

There's a related story about Mahatma Gandhi that comes to mind: once a woman from a small town went to Mahatma Gandhi and asked him to tell her child to stop eating so much candy. Gandhi asked the woman to come back in two weeks with her child. She did so and brought her child back to Gandhi who turned and plainly told the child that he should not eat candy because it was not good for him. The woman there after asked him why he had told her to take a somewhat difficult trip back and forth in two weeks when he could earlier have told her child this same message. Mahatma Gandhi answered that two weeks ago he himself was eating candy. He said he had to stop eating candy so that his words would carry weight.

The same is true for Dr. Fred. His words ring true. His nutritional advice is tangibly inspiring because he thoroughly lives what he teaches. You can feel it.

Quite simply, everyone I have referred to him over the years who complied with his advice returned to good health. He is a rare human being and altruistic healer. I admire his integrity and sincerity and offer my highest praise to a talented, dedicated and gentle man. Dr. Fred has enriched my own life in many ways. I am happy to pay tribute to this remarkable healer.

Michael Saiber, President, Vision/E3Live

Dedication & Acknowledgements

This book is dedicated to all the people that God has put in my life who have helped me develop Your Healthy Journey since my birth in 1929. They are too numerous to mention by name, but they are all in my thoughts and prayers.

Special thanks go to Rory Dean for all his help and for offering the constant encouragement that made this book possible.

I thank Clarisse Domingo for her devotion to the truth, Jonathan Collins for editing this book, in special memory to Enrique Candioti for his art direction and friendship, Larry Law for all his skills, Joseph Serpico for his feedback, Michael Perrine for bringing the message to others, and Michael Saiber and Tamara Campbell of Vision and E-3 Live for their warm friendship and hospitality, and to my wife Alma, my daughters, Renee and Robyn, whose talents and gifts were always there.

I also dedicate this book to the tens of thousands of people who have had the courage to set out on Your Healthy Journey. Often they were in the midst of a crisis or tragedy, and yet they were able to accomplish the seemingly impossible task of transforming their lives, realizing their God-given remedial healing capabilities, and achieving true health in body, mind, and spirit.

In conclusion, whatever % of a raw food lifestyle you choose to live by from 60% to 100% (most do 70/30) when done correctly will give you longevity and health, so finally, I give thanks to the creation of the human body.

The human body is a Divine spirit, mind & body: **Induced, Driven & Expressed.** *The health of the physical body is spiritually & vibrationally* **induced**, *electrically & chemically* **driven**, *and biologically* **and genetically expressed.**

Fred Bisci, PhD

THE GIFT

To some he is healer, to me he is dad,
He might have brought you comfort,
Which could have been your health
For you that was a fortune
For me that is my family treasure.

He has a wife for three decades more,
Two daughters, which he does adore
Two dogs that help create him
At the very core.

This all means love
Love to be given, love to spread far
Whether family, friends or client
His arm will reach your hand,
His heart will reach your soul
His words will reach your mind
What an understatement to say, "Kind"

With the age of eighty drawing near,
His life has been so dear
With one dedication,
With many different forms
A commitment to care,
At it's true nature hard to bare.
One man that has to be many
How much can one give,
Never did he run empty
He would say, "I am a man of plenty".

Knowledge is one thing required for his journey.
The gift to give,
the nature to be concerned,
the instinct to love.
That is a miracle, one not to be kept a secret
But a pleasure to share.

I've witnessed this for thirty years
Thankful for my close view
Now it's your turn
Let's see what this gift can do for you.

Robyn Bisci

Table of Charts

EATING GUIDELINES

Organically Grown Produce & Real Fresh Foods 96-97

DETAILS OF WHAT TO PUT IN 98-99

RECIPES

Delicious Juices & Delightful Salads... 100-101

FOOD COMBINING CHART 105

YOUR HEALTHY JOURNEY FRED'S FOOD PYRAMID............................... 106

INTERMEDIATE LEVEL LIFESTYLE/MENU - 3 MEALS/DAY...................... 110-111

ADVANCED LEVEL RAW LIFESTYLE/MENU—2/3 MEALS/DAY 112

Disclaimer:

Your Healthy Journey does not dispense medical advice. Your Healthy Journey does not recommend the use of any product or technique as a replacement or substitute for medical treatment for physical, medical or psychological conditions without the advice of a physician.

Your Healthy Journey does not claim to diagnose or cure any ailments physical or psychological. The intent of Your Healthy Journey is to offer information of a general nature to help your quest for physical, emotional and spiritual wellbeing.

In the event you use any of this information for yourself or others, Your Healthy Journey assumes no responsibility and specifically denies any and all liability.

Table of Contents

DEDICATION & ACKNOWLEDGEMENTS i

THE GIFT v

ABOUT THE AUTHOR 1

HEALTH IS YOUR WEALTH 3

PART I - The Principles

1. What You Leave Out 13
2. What You Put In. 23
3. Times, Sequences and Combinations 29
4. Overeating 33
5. Trust Your Body 37
6. Cellular Gases 43
7. Cleansing & Detoxification 49
8. Sleep, Rest, & Exercise. 59
9. Individual Differences. 61
10. Eat to Live. 63
11. Mind, Body, Spirit. 65

PART II - The Plan

1. Setting Lifetime Parameters. 71
2. Juices and Salads 75
3. Balancing The Scale. 77
4. Core Products & Living Foods 83
5. The General Rules 89
6. Eating Guidelines. 96
7. Details of What To Put In 98
8. Recipes. 100
9. Food Combining 103
10. Intermediate Level Lifestyle/Menu 107

PART III - The Process

Healing & Regeneration. 117

PART IV - The Practice

The Foundation. 131

APPENDIX

Daily Meditations 140
Food For Your Thoughts. 142

QUESTIONS & ANSWERS 147

THE PRODUCTS 158

FREDDY'S THOUGHTS 169

"WELCOME TO YOUR HEALTHY JOURNEY"

About the Author

D r. Fred Bisci, born, 1929, has a PhD in Nutritional Science and has run an active, pioneering practice in New York City for over fifty years. Dr. Bisci has helped over 35,000 people all over the world with numerous health issues. He does this by guiding them into a change through their eating and drinking lifestyles using the **Real Fresh Food Approach**.

His outlook is unique, not from a dietary or nutritional standpoint but from a biochemical appreciation of how the multiple variables in the human body directly relate to the attention that is paid to **what we leave out** of our lifestyle, followed by **what we put in**.

Dr. Bisci's clinical experience and knowledge has repeatedly demonstrated that making a commitment to lifestyle changes is the key to optimal health. Dr. Bisci has also found that there is a correlation between the long-term effects of processed foods, overeating and the acceleration of the aging process. His approach involves freshly prepared plant-based foods and food combinations of fresh vegetables and fruits, along with cooked portions to meals. It is based on the principle that the body is self-healing. When we leave out toxic, processed foods from our lifestyle and put in Real, Fresh Foods, we release our body's God-given ability to always seek health.

Dr. Bisci hosted his own television show, *Eat Your Way to Health,* which had the largest viewing TV audience in New York City and won the famed Nova award for best TV health series. He has been interviewed and quoted in numerous books, health periodicals, and radio and TV shows. He has also spoken nationally and internationally at universities, professional organizations, and business groups on "How to lead a Healthy Life". He has also worked with amateur and professional weightlifters, boxers, basketball, football and baseball players, marathon runners, tri-athletes, wrestlers, and actors.

Dr. Bisci was born in 1929. He has completed eighteen marathons and two ultra-thons. He also has a history as a Navy boxing champ and has practiced Olympic-style power weight lifting and still leads an athletic life. He has been happily married for over thirty years, with two lovely daughters and a constant friend to all types of animals.

Health Is Your Wealth

The United States of America, which has for many years been proud of its self-proclaimed status as the "greatest country in the world", is in a state of tragic decline. Walk down any street, peer into any store or café, pay a visit (Heaven forbid!) to an all-you-can-eat buffet at a Las Vegas casino, and all the evidence you need is there, staring you in the face.

I'm not referring to the state of our economy, our wars, our politics, our debt or any of the dozens of other controversial topics that could justifiably be mentioned. I'm talking about the nation's health. If you have the eyes to see, what you will observe is a people whose physical vitality is rapidly waning: many of us are dangerously overweight, our bodies have been poisoned by processed "foods", and our society is plagued by degenerative diseases that were rarities in previous generations but have now become commonplace.

How many people do you know who are suffering or have died from cancer or heart disease? What are your chances of escaping a similar fate? Some researchers predict that over the next ten years 25% of all men will be diagnosed with prostate cancer. That's one out of every four men. Women don't fare any better, since statistics for contracting breast cancer are of the same order of magnitude. This is just one form of one disease. Do a calculation based on all types of cancer and heart disease; add in the other common degenerative diseases, and it goes up to 75%. The future of our society looks bleak.

Worse still, it is not just our bodies that are degenerating. The mind, body, and spirit are all interdependent, and when one of them is in decline, so are the others, whether or not it is apparent on the surface. Therefore, our ailing bodies are a sure indicator that emotionally and spiritually we're in trouble too. Look around you again, and you'll see the signs everywhere.

That's the bad news. Fortunately, there is also some very good news: The remedy for this dreadful state of affairs is simple. Notice that **I said 'simple', not 'easy'**. It's *simple* because it can be stated in a couple of sentences: "Stop consuming toxic foods that are not suited to the Biochemical make-up of your body, and instead return to a natural original lifestyle composed primarily of raw fruits, vegetables, nuts, seeds, and sprouts. Eat these plant-based foods dominantly raw, in the correct combinations and sequences, and avoid over-eating." But it isn't *easy* because doing these simple things runs counter to ingrained habits, addictions, vested interests on the part of corporations, and our reluctance as a society to work for long-term rather than short-term goals.

I've been striving for 50 years to open people's minds and hearts to the simple truths that I will be telling you in this book. During that time I have studied lifestyle, food and nutritional science in great detail, gathered my data by working with tens of thousands of clients, and, above all, used my own body as a living laboratory. What I'm going to tell you is true, its effectiveness has been demonstrated time and time again, and it will work for you if you allow it to. I'm not going to promise that you'll live to the age of 120 with no illness, though such an outcome *is* possible. What I can say is that, though genetic and environmental factors may limit what you can achieve, if you apply the principles in this book "Your Healthy Journey" you will live longer and enjoy far better health—in mind, body and spirit—than you will do if you continue with your current habits.

This applies if you (or someone you love) are battling a life-threatening illness. I cannot guarantee that the lifestyle I'm going to propose will save you, but I can tell you that I have worked with a large number of supposedly fatally ill people who have recovered by embarking on Your Healthy Journey. It's likely, though not certain, that you or your loved-one will have the same outcome.

Your part is simply to decide that you want to deal with the root cause of premature aging and ill health. But this is a lot harder than it sounds. First, you have to overcome the ingrained habits I mentioned earlier. These include the habits you formed in childhood, when you associated certain foods with love and safety. These foods may be slowly poisoning you, but you may be reluctant to eliminate them if they bring you emotional comfort. There are also habits to do with taste: for most people something only seems tasty if it is very salty or very sweet.

But this is simply an illusion caused by the body's remarkable ability to adapt. If you remove salt and refined sugars from your diet, your meals will at first taste bland and unappetizing. However, as your palate becomes accustomed to the reduced stimulation, you will gradually start to detect and appreciate a symphony of new flavors that you never noticed before. It's like walking in the desert in bright sunlight and then suddenly entering a palace. At first, you can barely see anything and cannot appreciate the beauty around you; but slowly you become accustomed to the less intense light and you start to see ornament sand decorations that delight you. Eventually the glare of the desert soon loses its appeal, and you want to spend more and more time in the palace.

In their most extreme form, your habits are addictions. You may have witnessed someone trying to break a drug habit, and seen how hard that can be, even when the individual knows that his addiction is killing him. Breaking an addiction to a diet composed of an abundance of junk food, sugars, saturated fats, and processed proteins is not, on the biochemical level, that different. The detoxification symptoms, fortunately, are much less severe, but the physiological principles involved are the same.

The next obstacle you have to overcome has been erected by corporations and special interest groups. Examine the situation honestly and you will discover that most of your attitudes towards food are a result of indoctrination by organizations who want you to buy their products, and spend billions of dollars a year to ensure that you do. "But what about the objective information provided by scientific research and impartial medical organizations?" you may ask. "Can't I trust that?" No, maybe not. Who do you think funded that research or those organizations? Look into it, and you will find out their interest and if you want to participate. Even though the dollar is a driving force in this country, and profit may be far more important than your health, remember you ultimately make the final decision. Please make it wisely!

Finally, you have to deal with our collective obsession with quick fixes rather than fulfilling a lasting lifestyle change. For example your body is aging! Then you have plastic surgery or Botox injections. Your teeth are falling out?

Get implants. You're obese? Have gastric bypass surgery. You have a malignant tumor? Kill it with chemicals or radiation. Your arteries are clogged? Angioplasty will take care of that. And so it goes on.

Very few medical doctors are interested in the underlying causes of your ailments. Why? Because it pays to treat symptoms. Pharmaceutical companies can't patent fruits and vegetables, so there is no financial incentive to prescribe them. Surgeons make no money if, instead of an operation, you allow your body naturally to potentially unblock your arteries by drinking green vegetable juices and adopting a dominant raw food plant-based lifestyle. In fact, the entire medical establishment and all the businesses that depend on it would come crashing down, if enough people took charge of their own health and tackled their problems at the source.

I'm not accusing doctors and businesses of premeditated skullduggery. It's just human nature to conduct your affairs according to your own self interest. Rather than blaming the professionals and corporations who are pulling the wool over our eyes, we need to become determined to see what's going on for ourselves and make a commitment to a decision that benefits us. It is truly very easy to do. We have to stop assuming that what the "experts" say is true, and investigate the matter for ourselves. We don't need any qualifications, money, or special knowledge. All we need is a small dose of common sense, an open mind, and the willingness to do a little experimentation and have faith in our healing capabilities.

In this regard, I have more good news to report: I believe that society is beginning to move in the right direction. What's happening today is parallel to the Renaissance in the 15th century, which was the beginning of the illumination of the mind. The peasants in Europe were kept under the dominion of the church and the aristocracy, and were not aware that they were being programmed and deceived by the information that was fed to them, and were being kept in darkness. They did not realize that they were being deprived of the sovereignty and freedom that was their birthright as human beings. They were really just beast of burdens that had most of the fruits of their labors taken away from them, and were convinced that this was their lot in life.

All this changed on the day that Martin Luther printed a proclamation and pinned it on the church door of Wittenberg Castle in Germany. He exposed the prevailing orthodox and the aristocracy's view and urged people to free themselves from the yoke of the church. He proclaimed that people were entitled to dignity and personal freedom, and as a result of this proclamation he was excommunicated from the church. He encouraged people to seek and educate themselves so they could open their minds and become enlightened. Well, the aristocracy reacted by imposing severe restrictions and punishments on those who tried to do this.

Later on, when Guttenberg invented the printing press, The stirred numbers of citizens rebelled and demanded their rights and their own opportunity to learn how to read and educate themselves about different subjects that were needed for them to become enlightened human beings. Again, the land barons and the church tried to prevent this from happening.

Something analogous to this is occurring in our time. Those in positions within the medical establishment and its collateral businesses are obscuring important information about the body's physiological healing that, if known by the average person, would transform his or her life. The main focus I have seen is that the human body has amazing, God given remedial capabilities. The body has the ability, under the right circumstances (that we can create with simple lifestyle changes), to regenerate, heal, prevent most of the diseases that afflict us today and live a high quality of life possible for a lifetime.

America has many of the best scientists and researchers in the world, and yet we are paradoxically one of the sickest industrialized countries. Just as people were kept in darkness until the 15th century, so too have we been kept in a certain amount of darkness concerning fundamental truths that should be part of our mainstream education in the field of health and well being. However, I believe we are on the verge of a new era, for many well informed people are now attempting to bring the information out into the open and into the mainstream. It has been difficult to establish credibility because, when deceit has prevailed for so long, the truth is perceived as something radical, and is thus rejected out of hand. Yet, the tide is definitely turning.

Many people over the last 60 years, myself included, have lived by these principles of a dominant or 100% raw food lifestyle, and the results indicate beyond a shadow of a doubt that poor dietary routines causes the majority of diseases and that a healthy lifestyle prevents them. I have seen countless numbers of people, who changed their nutritional lifestyle and had the courage to be willing participants in their own recovery, accomplish unbelievable health and quality of life beyond their thoughts. The results happen so quickly and dramatically that they seem like miracles.

But if you go back a few decades, all of this was commonplace. When I was a little boy growing up in the 30s and 40s, the people I knew rarely were sick. We were all born at home and were fed real, organic foods grown by my mother and other families in a very large garden. Whatever else we ate came from a store where the grains were whole and the fruits and vegetables were unsprayed and untouched—they actually still had dirt on them. I don't even remember as a boy ever seeing a doctor until I was able to go out and buy some penny candy. (Fortunately I never had a lot of pennies, so I seldom had the chance to indulge myself.) We typically all grew up to be healthy young adults, till technology took us in a new direction of scientific processing and devitalization of our food. Looking back, I recall many people who, provided they did not die of infectious diseases at a young age, were able to remain in good health and go on to live to a ripe old age.

Today it is very different. You walk into a huge supermarket with thousands of varieties of food available, and if you have the money, you can indulge yourself without limit. However, the majority of these foods are processed packaging and, in the long run, unfit for human health and consumption. The transition has been so gradual that we have unknowingly slipped into this bleak situation. But we can break free of it. We can unmask the deceptions behind these foods, whose purpose is not to promote health and well being but to enrich corporate profits. Please make your decisions, wisely!

What I would like to do in this book is to help you understand the appalling effects of our industrialized diets and show you how to change your lifestyle in a way that will make you a much healthier, happier, and a more spiritually aware person. However, it is crucial that you are a willing participant in your own change and are determined to achieve a state of health and well being beyond what most people imagine is possible.

Knowing that any effort you make will be rewarded a thousand times over. Once you start on Your Healthy Journey!

PART I

The Principles

1. What You Leave Out

NATURAL LAW

As a country we are getting sicker, even though we have the most advanced medical technology in the world. The reason for this is that technology treats symptoms not causes. The cause of 85% of degenerative diseases in this country is poor standard of living, in particular our diet, but rather than changing our lifestyle, we look for quick fixes. One of the hardest changes to face is the emotion adjustments from leaving out toxic, processed foods and a person's overall addiction to pleasure. But in order to make a lifestyle change and come close to our full potential, we must submit, faithfully, to natural laws and the complex order of God's created human design. If you jump out of a plane without a parachute, you are subject to the laws of aerodynamics and gravity; in spite of thinking you're a canary, you're going to hit the ground. True lasting health is a natural law and letting the healing function take place is the unleashing of this kind of process in the human body.

The body's biochemistry evolved over millions of years, whereas our current dietary lifestyles developed over the last hundred years. One of the laws governing the body is that it will only function optimally if what we eat is consistent with our biochemical make-up. This is so obvious, you'd think most people would understand and act in accord. The reason they don't see the obvious is that the body has an extraordinary capacity to adapt to toxic foods and to desensitize itself, so that people are not aware of what's actually happening to them. So let's become aware.

BODY AWARENESS

Our desensitization can reach mind-boggling extremes: for example, a two hundred and seventy-five pound woman was admitted to the hospital after she complained about indigestion pains. Two hours later, she gave birth to a child. She had no idea that she had been pregnant. Another example: An elderly man complained about a continual dull headache for weeks. He went to a doctor who asked him about his habits, activities, and so on. Upon repeated questioning, it was determined that the man had not had a bowel movement in weeks. He was not even aware that he was constipated and that this might be the source of his headache.

We might find such stories amazing, but everyone is like this to some extent. Most people today have such a low level of body awareness that they do not realize they are suffering from poor health until a severe blow lays them out for the count. Indeed, it is this absence of consciousness that permits the body to degenerate in the first place, because when a person is attentive to their body's needs, they become aware when something is going wrong and make the necessary changes before disaster strikes.

Increasingly good health has the effect of increasing our awareness of the body. As the major aches and pains disappear, we become more sensitive to all the body's needs. The minor irritations that were not noticed previously may now enter our awareness. For example, suppose you have a slight headache and, at the same time, you are suffering from a violently bleeding ulcer that causes you to vomit every two or three hours. Do you think you will notice the headache? No, you'll be too busy worrying about the ulcer to pay any attention to the other minor pain. After the ulcer is gone however, you might suddenly realize, "My head hurts!"

This is exactly what happens when the body goes through its healing process. As you regain health, you become more aware of the minor pains that may have plagued you for years but have been around for so long that you've grown used to them. It's not that your increasing health has given your body any new pains; they were just unnoticed.

This new sensitivity is a blessing. Now your body can tell you what it needs, what to avoid, and what habits to discontinue and leave out. If you have stopped eating meat, for instance, your body will become more sensitive to the harmful effects and pressure of such food has on the human body. If you were to eat that same food again, you might become sick or have a detox/cleansing effect. As you become compatible with this new body chemistry from the commitment of Your Healthy Journey, the food you could tolerate before from your old chemistry is not compatible with the new and improved more efficient chemistry. This is the body's way of saying, "That stuff's no good for me, and I'm strong enough now to let you know."

Body awareness is one of the first great gifts of health. This new feeling should not be mistaken for morbid sensitivity. It is your guardian angel that will guide you past the pitfalls of poor foods, unhealthy practices, and other life destroying habits and experiences.

DIETS

The standard American diet is one that we are all familiar with. People are consuming processed foods and drinks, such as box and can foods, pizza, hamburgers, hot dogs, and soda; once in a while, they have a baby token salad.

Society is now starting to realize that this is not conducive to good health, quality of life and longevity.

There is also a plethora of fad diets. For example, high protein diets have been in vogue because they are very effective for losing weight, but they can lead to various problems. When you are eating this type of diet you're usually eating too few carbohydrates and greens, which means your diet is too low in fiber and you will suffer from constipation. Add inadequate consumption of water to this, and you will suffer from constant constipation and possible open the pathways to serious diseases.

Another problem is that this high protein diet is very acidic. A healthy blood and tissue pH should be about 7.3 to 7.4. The urine and saliva pH should be between 6.8 and 7.2. On a high protein diet, you will move out of the healthy pH range and this can put a burden on your kidneys. The body will also leach alkaline salts—calcium and magnesium out of your skeletal frame, which can lead to osteoporosis. And even though your cholesterol level may decrease, living this type of diet will lead to an increase in inflammatory diseases. It also raises your consumption of non- essential fat, which can have serious consequences. What's more, you become very sensitive to carbohydrates. So if you lose 50 pounds on the diet, come off it, and go back to eating carbohydrates, you'll not only regain all the weight you lost, you'll probably gain a lot more.

Also, this type of diet speeds up your metabolism, which results in an acceleration of the aging process or abnormal cell growth. It's like taking a new car with a never-ending supply of gasoline, by taking a normal engine idle and then putting a cinder block on the gas pedal so that the engine races continuously. This is analogous to your metabolism speeding along and racing your body engine all the time with a high protein diet. Although, you do burn calories faster, and that is why you lose weight, but in the process of doing that you are putting more wear and tear on your internal organs—your kidneys and your liver specifically.

Another approach would be the Macrobiotic diet, which has a number of benefits and has allowed many people to improve their quality from different illnesses. Apart from a moderate consumption of fish, there is little animal protein in the regime. They also advocate eating brown rice, sea vegetables and some fermented foods. This is not a diet where you eat tremendous amounts of food, and so some people have done well on it.

The Zone Diet also has some virtues. It regulates the amount of protein and carbohydrate you eat and proposes a good variety of different foods.

Then there's the Natural Hygiene diet, which consists of water fasting, fruits, vegetables, nuts, seeds, and avocados but juicing and blending your food, cleansing and super greenfoods is not recommended. This worked well for some people but not everybody because it was not enough and they ran into serious health problems. These deficiencies were pointed out by Dr. Christopher Gian-Cursio, who tried to enlighten the Natural Hygiene community about making the necessary changes and understanding the broader view of variables that make a complete lifestyle but they couldn't accept the criticism.

Given this deluge of diet programs and diet gurus, you are likely to end up bewildered. Perhaps the challenge of sorting through them, and finding that they are often diametrically opposed to one another, will make you gravitate to the Eat Right for Your Type diet, which proposes different dietary regimes according to your blood type. "Finally," you exclaim, "here's a program that makes the decision for me!" But I have to tell you it is a poor decision.

An additional source of confusion is that most dietary programs, as a group, do achieve positive results. How can such a thing be possible? If the body is subject to Natural Law, how can it respond positively to a low protein vegetarian, plant-based lifestyle and yet also apparently do well on a high-protein meat diet? The answer is that most diets have one common denominator—they encourage you to eliminate the toxic, stimulating processed foods and drinks that are so destructive to human physiology. They also encourage you to stop over-eating. So, in the short term, exclusion rather than inclusion is the key, and many diets will at first make you feel and look better because they succeed with the part of the equation that is "**what you leave out**." In the long term, however, those same regimes will harm your health because the foods they encourage you to include in the diet are not consistent with the body's true requirements. When it comes to **what you put in,** no foods compare in quality to raw fruits, vegetables, nuts, seeds and sprouts which alkalinize, energize, nourish, and oxygenate the body in an optimal manner.

WHAT YOU SHOULD LEAVE OUT

Most people think when they open up their box of cold cereal in the morning, that this food is the same as the food that it originated from. (We somehow forget that corn and wheat don't grow out of the ground in the form of flakes.) Many people are also under the misconception that food that is prepared as a canned, boxed, cartoned or microwave food/drink product is done typically in a three-stage procedure and people believe that it is the same as the way that nature gives it to us in its original form. If it still looks the same it is the same concept.

When you take fruit, for instance, and you cook it, include additives and/or preservatives, put it in a can and then add sugar to it, even though it tastes good, no way it compares to when you're eating a piece of fresh fruit. In fact, most of the vital energy and companion nutrients of the original fruit have been processed out and your body doesn't get full value of it as fruit anymore. Likewise, when you boil vegetables in water, you render them nutritionally inadequate, especially if you then can or freeze them. The same is true when you remove the bran and germ from grains, or bleach flour; although you're making them more readily available, you are decreasing their vitality from a nutritional standpoint.

Any food/drink or meat product that has chemicals added to it to preserve it or make it grow bigger or became heavier, is a substance that is far more harmful than most people suspect. The situation is serious when it comes to fruits and vegetables, but it's a national crisis when it comes to animal products, which are full of hormones and antibiotics that are directly linked as a potential factor to cancer and other serious diseases.

So what you should leave out of your lifestyle, or at least reduce to a minimum, is:

Processed Foods. A processed food is something that you can't see or find in nature. The more highly processed food is, the less it looks like something you could theoretically grow in your garden. Typical, highly processed cooked foods at breakfast are: pasteurized orange juice, packaged cereals, sugar, commercial breads and other baked goods. At lunch: sandwiches, french fries, ice cream, and sodas. At dinner: pasta, canned sauces, pies and pastries.

Non-Organic Foods. Some people think the interest in Organic produce and meats is a fad with no genuine basis to it; but that is absolutely not true. In our society, commercially grown foods are laden with pesticides, herbicides, additives, and hormones; these chemicals easily overwhelm and overwork your liver and kidneys, requiring them to perform functions that the body's chemistry and physiology were never intended, especially if you're looking for quality health and longevity. The average healthy liver weighs between 3 to 3½ pounds; but many people in our culture eat such toxic amounts of food that their livers weigh 4 to 4½ pounds. So organically grown produce is not just a frill or a fad; it's an essential part of Your Healthy Journey.

Many people don't trust the regulations that control organically grown produce; however, in my experience most of the time you can depend upon them. People also question if the taste is better. This may be true for them in the beginning, because until you move to a cleansing, healthy nutritional lifestyle, your palate is dull. But when your taste buds become more sensitive, you will discover that organically grown fruits and vegetables generally taste far better. Also because of the lack of chemicals and the way they're grown, they won't last as long, but they are much better for you.

Alcohol/Coffee. These drinks overload your liver and kidneys and acidify your body, and Your Healthy Journey will progress more swiftly without them.

Start by eliminating these foods and you will immediately see results. Whenever you make a change, the body responds, either moving backwards or forwards. When you learn how to stop moving backwards, your body will continuously move forward to becoming an ongoing potential towards health. Once you have this understanding, you have the ability to live a life that is glorious, far beyond what most people realize.

So next time you go into the local supermarket, you may wonder if there's anything in the store that you can eat. The regrettable truth is that most of the shelves are filled with processed, unnatural products that do not qualify as Real, Fresh Foods. When you clean out your mind, body and spirit, and your vision becomes clear, you will walk into a supermarket and instead of seeing a cornucopia of foods, you will see rows of inert products that have little or no **vital force** left in them.

One exception to this is the produce department. Increasing numbers of supermarkets are stocking organic fruits and vegetables, and if you're lucky enough to live near one that does, this is a good starting point for Your Healthy Journey. Moreover, supermarkets respond to consumer demand, and so the more often you and others buy organic fruit and vegetables, the more choice you will have in the future.

In most parts of the country, there are farmer's markets where you can buy fresh, locally-grown organic fruits and vegetables. If not, there are often cooperatives that you can join. If you have a high quality natural organic food store near you, that can be a good option also.

If you're unable to find a good selection of organic produce, then buy what you can or otherwise eat conventionally grown foods as a temporary measure. Conventional farmers are beginning to spray less, and so some non-organic food is not as toxic as it used to be but keep on looking for organic because I have always found good sources for organic produce and plant-based foods. You just have to be a good detective, it's out there.

The main idea is to do the best you can, without becoming obsessive. Always remember the body is extremely adaptable and consequently you have a 20% margin of error—meaning that without doing everything perfectly, you can still achieve progressive results. Nevertheless, do eat organic whenever possible, because it maximizes your chances of success and it makes a statement that you want not only a healthy body but also a healthy world—for yourself and for the generations coming after you.

Congratulations, you are now resting securely on the *First Foundation* of good health: **what you leave out**. Now you can move to the second foundation: **what you put in,** eating from the garden of **Real, Clean, Fresh Foods**.

2. What You Put In

My work aims not to offer yet another dietary theory but rather to discover what the truth really is. The mindset for example is that certain biological factors exist that cannot be changed; people resolve themselves to that's who we are and how we were created. Many diets ignore these factors because of the tendency in our culture to want the best of both worlds—to be healthy, happy and have a lean body without eating truly healthy foods. **But that just doesn't work.**

Fortunately, it seems that our society is now ready to move toward a more holistic view of health and wellness. Many people have begun to appreciate the connection between lifestyle/food and preventative care, and they are willing to take charge of their own health. My purpose is to provide the information that will help the public make wise lifestyle choices based on facts and experience, rather than fads and wishful-thinking to what it really is!

FOODS TO EAT

My approach involves an all raw or predominantly raw food lifestyle with an option, if chosen, for moderate cooked portions with a meal, but my main focus is to examine health not from a nutritional standpoint but rather a biochemical one. As we saw in the previous chapter, there are many dietary programs that advocate different approaches then mine and still seem to give successful results. Yet, just because a diet appears to have succeeded in the short term, it doesn't mean it's an ideal strategy for the long term. On the contrary, the road to true improvement is often riddled with short-term setbacks, which the uninformed might view as failures. Even though these setbacks are uncomfortable, they are all part of the change our bodies must go through in order to regain optimal health. Systems that offer shortcuts or panaceas are not going to lead to lasting health and wellbeing.

When I first started down this path in my life, I decided I would explore these choices with my own body first and see where it led me. What I have come to conclude is that the optimal lifestyle choice for good health consists of:

Raw foods – organic fruits, vegetables, nuts, seeds, and sprouts –making up all or the major part of your lifestyle.

Carbohydrates – in small quantities.

Animal protein – moderate intake (or none at all).

What this means is that you should reduce the quantity of carbohydrates you consume in the form of grains and increase your consumption of fruits and vegetables. Ideally buy produce that is organic and recently picked because fruits and vegetables start to oxidize the minute they have been harvested, and by the time they make it to the supermarket they have lost 50-75% of their nutrients. If they are not organic and have been lying on the shelf for a while, very few nutrients remain.

Though a moderate intake of grains is acceptable, you should, however, eliminate entirely all *processed* grains (where the bran and the germ has been removed), which are junk foods, harm your health and wear down your body. In other words, eat whole grains. If you eat rice, for example, choose brown rice. Also try to avoid grains that contain gluten—wheat, rye, oats, and barley—because gluten becomes a sticky substance in your digestive system. Choose instead brown rice, millet, buckwheat or quinoa.

Regarding protein, reduce your intake of animal products and buy grass-fed meat, free-range chicken or turkey, and fresh wild fish, organic if possible. Even though a plant-based lifestyle, as raw as possible, is the best way to go, I believe you are better off over your lifetime taking gradual steps so there are no dramatic effects and you can build your level of confidence as you move along.

AN ALL-RAW FOOD LIFESTYLE

I personally have eaten only raw plant foods for over 50 years with phenomenal results. There is no doubt that an all-raw lifestyle is the ultimate approach, but I do not generally recommend it to my clients because very few of them would be capable of sustaining it over their lifetime. So a mainly raw food lifestyle provides excellent results and is a more realistic objective for most people. This is the reason I formulated the Intermediate Level Lifestyle because the worst thing for your health is to go 100% raw and bounce in and out of different lifestyle parameters. So heads up when you're on Your Healthy Journey because over a period of years you will get into problems going back and forth between the dominance of raw foods and cooked foods especially if you fall back to animal protein. It is better and more practical to adopt a mainly raw food lifestyle and stick to it than to attempt to go 100% raw and slip back and forth.

MARGIN OF ERROR

There is a certain margin of error while you're on Your Healthy Journey: if you have a 70% - 80% base of **Real, Fresh, Raw Plant, Foods** you can vary the remaining 30% - 20% of your meals with cooked portions, if done correctly you can still obtain optimal health. Some people want to be vegetarians while others are not willing to give up or still want animal protein. So whatever your parameters are, within reason, you can become healthy. Once you've determined the parameters, however, while giving your body a chance to react to the new chemistry, then you have to stick to it, the rest of your life. That's the key to an optimal eating lifestyle: not jumping in and out of your parameters, because vacillating in this way puts a huge strain on the body and will express your genetic weaknesses and we all have them.

QUALIFYING FOODS

When we are following parameters, we start by qualifying foods. This classification of foods is determined by what requires the most or least amount of energy and time to digest and assimilate foods.

When you consider the energy efficiency and time factors of different foods, **Real, Fresh Foods** are incomparably better than processed foods, especially if they are organic. These are complete foods. So when you're looking at the labels on packaged foods, pay attention to the amount of these ingredients. Do you recognize any wholesome ingredients such as fruits, vegetables, seeds, nuts or grains? How many chemical ingredients are listed? These are all factors that are associated with the time and energy your body's biochemistry requires in order to deal with these chemical variables. The fewer artificial ingredients in packaged foods, if you must eat them, the less strain it has on the body.

Highly processed food has been industrialized and distorted from its original food state and is no longer viewed by the body's biochemistry as a real and wholesome food. Most packaged and processed foods are broken up, rearranged and altered with added chemicals and preservatives. They have lost their companion nutrients that made them a whole food. Then the liver has to deal with all these rearranged and altered chemicals and the liver is a very important organ that performs over 500 different functions. The main function is that of a filter. The liver will have to work harder and spend more time to deal with altered foods that are not in their original food state. Depending on the quantity of processed foods you consume and your genetic predisposition, you will finally get to a point where your liver will no longer be able to deal with the insult and become overwhelmed. Then chemical residues will be stored in your liver or somewhere in your body—it could be anywhere in your cells—and will hinder your body's ability to function at its peak performance. When you have a lifestyle consisting of processed and concentrated foods, this will cause an intoxicating exogenous effect on the human body. This is the precursor to loss of health, low quality of life, and diminished well being.

3. Times, Sequences and Combinations

FREQUENCY OF MEALS

How often to eat has become a very confusing issue today. Even well-known nutritionists sometimes advocate what is in reality a major dietary mistake. Since the advent of high-protein diets (another mistake) many people are eating six meals a day and consuming animal proteins three or four times a day.

In the beginning, they feel well from the stimulating effect of the animal protein and credit the animal protein for keeping their blood sugar level stable but when you have a history of consuming frequent meals of animal protein and then reduce your amounts what you may interpret as low blood sugar may in most cases be the experience of detoxification.

So, there are three issues to consider here: First, the virtue of maintaining blood sugar levels by snacking is only (somewhat) valid if your diet is high in processed carbohydrates which creates insulin spikes followed by low blood sugar levels, in which case it is advisable to raise them again. But why correct a 'wrong' with a 'wrong'? The healthy choice is to turn the first 'wrong' into a 'right' and establish an eating lifestyle that maintains stable blood sugar levels between meals and create health rather than instability.Second, snacking leads to food fermenting in the intestinal digestive tract and cravings, because the previous snack, still only partially digested, impedes the progress of the food following it.

Third, and most importantly, snacking prevents the body from going through a detoxification process, which it must do on a **daily basis** if a person is to live a long and healthy life. By eating six meals a day, you never give your stomach a chance to empty out, and so your body is unable to detoxify and keep you efficient on a cellular level.

So typically, after a meal, don't eat again until your stomach is completely empty. If you get into the habit of putting food on top of half-digested food throughout the day, or you eat late at night, you will trigger the body's fermentation process, which acidifies the body and causes inflammation. This is serious because all degenerative diseases (arthritis, muscular dystrophy, cancer, etc), in fact all diseases, period—start with inflammation on a cellular level and this adds to a burden on the body. This has been known for a long time by certain eminent scientists. Two hundred years ago, Virchow, the father of pathology, asserted that all disease commences with injury and inflammation to the cell. In 1934, Nobel laureate Otto Warburg stated cancer was caused by "fermentative non-oxidative respiration" which is the precursor to inflammation and not necessarily related to whole food sugars. So it is my belief that after 60 years of clinically working with people and living Your Healthy Journey inflammation is the cause of most diseases.

In my experience, eating six meals a day, though it might make you feel stronger in the short term, is likely to take a heavy toll on your health in the long run. For optimal health, you should not eat more than three meals a day. I'm aware of the fact that many people may differ with me about this, but the bottom line is results. Over the course of the last fifty years, I've advised tens of thousands of clients about the negative consequences of grazing all throughout the day on solid food, and those who have followed my advice have achieved wonderful results.

SEQUENCES AND FOOD COMBINING

To maximize the energy available to you and achieve optimum health, you need to practice eating foods in the correct order and combination. If you fail to follow the principles of food combining and sequencing, and if you over eat, you may not immediately notice the negative consequences on the body, but they will be occurring nevertheless. The reason for this is that you will be using a great deal of your energy to break down the food, absorb it, and turn it into more energy for the body. Compare this with the smaller amount of energy that you'll use if your digestive process operates optimally. You will see that poor eating habits result in a significant loss of energy that could be used for healing, sports performance, mental functioning, and so on. For example, if your body is battling a serious disease like cancer, and you deprive it of 50-60% of its energy, it's obvious that you will seriously reduce your chances of recuperating.

The principle of correct sequencing is that more rapidly digested and less energy output foods should be eaten first then more slowly digested foods second. This means that salads are eaten before meat or fish, raw foods before cooked foods. Fruits should ideally be eaten on their own. The reason for this is that if easily digested foods are blocked in the digestive tract by previous concentrated or cooked foods, which take more time to digest, then the easily digested foods will start to ferment.

The principle of correct combining is that different kinds of food require different types of digestion—for example starches and proteins. If you combine these foods in the same meal, you put a heavy burden on your digestive system and you may initiate the harmful process of fermentation. Therefore study the food combining chart in this book and eat compatible foods at different meals and leave out the incompatible foods within the same meal.

However, there are special circumstances, and what is right for one person may not be right for another. For example, if you follow the guidelines, you'll eat nuts after a salad, but some people don't easily digest the protein in nuts, and do better reversing the order or eating the two foods together. So experience how this works for you.

The point is, though you're trying to break old habits that keep you stuck in harmful eating patterns, do not go to the other extreme and become a fanatic. Listen to your body and learn from it. Also, if you can, talk to a professional and receive advice that is targeted to your individual physiology and chemistry needs.

Sometimes you may be afraid of feeling hungry if you eat this way. This may happen initially, but soon you will adjust to your new eating patterns and feel fine. Though it does take time, you can overcome the habit that makes you feel you need to snack continuously or combine as many foods as possible into one meal. The key is to eat three meals a day, let your stomach empty out between meals; observe the correct sequencing and combination of foods, and not to eat late or eat three hours before you go to bed. If you do that for a decent length of time, and stick to the parameters of Your Healthy Journey, any hunger pangs will soon disappear and you will experience your energy soaring and your mind will become clear—to an extent that you will find amazing.

4. Overeating

When I first became interested in raw foods, I expected people who eat mostly raw to be jogging round the block at the age of 90, but that was not the case. Many raw fooders were dying in their 70's and 80's, just like everybody else. There had to be something wrong, I realized, because the theoretical lifespan for a person living a healthy lifestyle is 120 years. Why aren't people on a raw food lifestyle living to the age of 100 or more?

I started looking for the answer by experimenting on myself, which I have continued to do for over 60 years. I began to realize that most people are eating more than their body needs; by **overeating**, we shorten our lifespan regardless of the quality of the food. I did an eight-year experiment on myself to discover if this was true. I ate low calorie, nutrient dense foods to see how long I could exist on this type of a lifestyle. I didn't set out to do it for eight years, and I was very surprised that it took me that long, but in the end I got my answer. I learned that systematic under-eating is the surest way of improving your health, giving both immediate and long-term results. When your body adjusts to systematic under-eating, it slows down your metabolic rate, which slows down the aging process and opens up the healing process. We have to remember the more you eat, the more you overeat. That is what most people experience but when you go on Your Healthy Journey you will be surprised because you'll be eating less food and at the same time getting all the nutrients you need.

But if you force yourself to systematically under-eat, and don't allow your body to adapt on a chemical level, you'll be undernourished. Keep in mind that your activity level will determine how many calories you really need. So all you need do is to avoid eating like it's a recreational sport, and your body will take care of the rest—your body chemistry will change and you will gradually require fewer calories and nutrients. While this is going on you're getting an adequate amount of calories that your body needs and getting enough protein. But this doesn't happen over night; it may take years for you to adapt completely.

How does the process work? When you eat mostly raw fresh foods correctly, and eliminate all processed foods, your body becomes an **amazingly efficient biological machine.**

Although during the first few years, you may feel better without changing the amount of food you eat, but after a period of time, if you continue to overeat, you are asking for problems. This is because when your chemistry changes on a cellular level and your blood gets cleaner, as it will do on raw foods over time, overeating places a burden on your body, which ultimately leads to the same problems other people have on an average diet. The cleaner you become and the more vitality you have, the faster you react to harmful or good foods and liquids associated with excessive consumption. Something you tolerated easily five years ago could make you very sick today or send you into a detox.

After eight years of under-eating, I finally decided to stop the experiment, not because I was encountering difficulties I was actually thriving, even though I was very slender—but just to see what would happen. Instantly, I started to experience some old health problems. I realized it was very dangerous for me to return to my former consumption of food.

Over the years, my understanding of this lifestyle/ nutritional principle has been confirmed with many different people: but it's certain that if you consistently eat mostly raw foods, eliminate processed foods, and do not over-eat, you'll have a fantastic amount of energy and great clarity of mind, which you will continue to enjoy even at an advanced age.

If you over consume animal protein, on the other hand, you will give the body strength but at the same time accelerate unintended cell growth and the aging process. If you look at different population groups around the world, you'll see that the people who eat the most animal protein have the least healthy lives and shortest life spans. So just because a person is strong enough to dead lift 700 lbs or run 20 miles does not mean he is healthy. (This doesn't mean you have to eliminate all animal protein completely in order to be on Your Healthy Journey because if you eat a small amount of meat preceding it by a large alkalinizing salad, you can do very well with it.)

The key to health and longevity is slowing down the aging process and building reserve vitality. Then, you don't have to exercise nearly as much in order to be very fit and vital; in fact you can exercise very little. Anybody who adopts a mostly raw food lifestyle over a relatively long period of time and gradually adjusts to letting their body eat less food, will find that they can go out and run 10 miles any time they feel like it, as if they've been training for weeks.

Try this and see for yourself. Let this book guide you and help you, but don't let it replace your own **experience.**

...most people are eating more than their body needs; by overeating, we shorten our lifespan regardless of the quality of the food.

5. Trust Your Body

Your body has tremendous remedial healing capabilities. Everything in the human body is chemical and everything is action and reaction. You do something; your body reacts—regardless of your intentions. You can eat something that your mind is certain is beneficial, and it will harm you; conversely, you can eat something you believe is harmful, and actually it can do you a lot of good. It all depends on the chemical reactions, not on what you think will happen.

We have what I believe is the body's God-given ability to be able to heal—that is if the obstacles to health and the impairment of the human physiology by a negative lifestyle are removed. These obstacles involve food, air, water, or any type of chemical, pesticide or poison that is introduced into the human body and even those introduced under the pretense of improving our lives or possible treating an illness.

Your body wants good health; it wants to be free from all pain and illness; it actively desires complete healing to take place within at all times. Your body is your friend and a partner in your effort to regain health but you have to work with it. The body has the innate capacity, knowledge, and wisdom to heal itself at anytime, if it is allowed to do so. The only thing we must do is to let the body conduct its work with as little interference as possible. We can furnish it with the highest quality food when it needs it, or withhold food when it does not desire it; we can exercise and rest the body, and give it fresh air and sunshine; other than that, all we can do is **be patient** and prudent, and not over-think the body's actions or become alarmed by its symptoms and try to suppress them. If you have any doubt seek professional advice.

However, the body is wise enough to accelerate the healing process to the maximum, when conditions permit. This may involve major cleansing efforts, when the body removes what it does not want, where literally pounds of old stored toxins are dumped into the blood stream to be eliminated, which can result in unpleasant symptoms.

If you trust your body's ability to heal itself, these symptoms become more bearable and are no longer a source of fear or misgiving. Ultimately, we must let our body perform its healthy restoring work at its own pace. We must believe that the body alone is capable of performing all the needed healing functions.

The dedication you apply to upgrading your eating and drinking habits will reveal remarkable results for the body and the mind. Amazing intelligence is present in every cell of the body; its multiple variables work together to manifest the remedial healing capabilities that are the potential of the human body. As you feed your body (**what you put in**) by following the **foundational** principles of **what you leave out**, the higher-quality foods give the cells an opportunity to discard and eliminate lower quality components (products to avoid) from the tissues. This makes room for the cells to utilize these higher-quality foods to rebuild and develop healthier tissue.

If we create optimum conditions for the body, it will always seek health on every level, from the overall macro-functions all the way down to the individual cell. We see this phenomenon in the self-healing nature of the body when it is confronted with colds, fevers, cuts, and swellings—in other words, illness and injury of any kind.

So what inhibits this natural healing process? Well, depriving the body of the optimum conditions by returning to your previous routines. This is why it cannot be overemphasized that you need to make a commitment to a lifestyle change and then live within your parameters; it is the only way your body can regain its health and maintain it throughout your lifetime.

PHASES OF ADAPTATION

Once you have made this commitment to Your Healthy Journey, you will experience challenging phases, which you might sometimes interpret as weakness or fatigue. You may be tempted to go back to your former routines, but remember the body needs time to adapt during the periods of chemical and physiological adjustment. When you realize this is a longer lifetime view, you understand why it is vital to allow a completion of these bodily actions every time that your body is going through a phase of adaptation. Do this and the rewards follow.

The first level of action when your body adapts is known as **Recuperation**. This initial phase should not take a long time, it could be several days or even weeks in some cases. It takes you through various stages to health during which the body changes its energy focus from the voluntary, peripheral, and external outside functions of your muscles and skin to the inner functions of the vital internal organs, where it starts the process of reconstruction. This change from the external to the internal produces a feeling of less energy in the muscles, which your mind understands as weakness. This lets you know that your internal organs need more energy and time for rebuilding; meanwhile there is less availability for muscular work. Any temporary feeling of weakness is not true weakness but a redeployment of the body's healing forces to more important areas. At this time, it is very important to get additional **rest and sleep**, and to conserve your energy.

It's easy to lose faith at this point. For example, you eat a large meal and then feel tired because your body requires more energy to perform its internal digestive functions. You interpret this as muscular weakness and fatigue, and so you decide to have a cup of coffee and dessert as a pick-up. This is a misinterpretation of the true situation. Listen carefully to your body, and it will tell you what's going on. The key is to develop the necessary understanding of your body's signals and you will push that dessert aside and in return get your just desserts in the form of improved health. So remember: **When your body speaks, Listen.**

During this phase of **Recuperation**, as you are following the parameters by choosing higher quality organic food (foods you should eat and drink), the cells get a chance to perform catabolism. Here the accent is on elimination by breaking down endogenous materials in the cells that have made life functions so burdensome. The body literally begins to clean house. It removes the garbage, discarding and eliminating lower quality processed/concentrated foods (products you should avoid) from all the tissues. At this juncture, the body's housecleaning causes the gross and immediate body wastes to be discarded more rapidly than new cells can be regenerated. You are like a fire that has been clogged with ashes; initially the ashes dampen your flame (your energy), but once they're removed the flame grows brighter than before.

One of the most noticeable outcomes of this *First Physical Phase,* **Recuperation** is weight loss that persists for a period of time. This will then be followed by the *Second Physical Phase* called **Stabilization,** in which the body's weight seeks to become balanced. As you continually follow your parameters, the amount of discarded wastes is now equal to the regeneration of cells. This stage persists for a while and is then followed by a *Third Physical Phase,* **Regeneration** which is the build-up period called **Anabolism**. Rest and sleep are the major promoters of the Anabolism phase and remember it's a free gift, don't forget to take it.

As the storage of energy increases, your weight starts to go up, even though you are consuming fewer calories. By consistently maintaining your lifestyle, improving the quality of the foods you consume, following the right eating and drinking mechanics, getting rest during the cleansing and detox process you facilitate the regeneration of cells, which improves digestion and assimilation.

As Your Healthy Journey continues, the body's need for the usual amounts of food decreases and you are able to maintain your weight and enjoy increased energy with less food. Most people follow the **Intermediate Level Menu Lifestyle** that is provided in this book. This is three meals a day—morning, noon and evening—although many individuals are able to function very efficiently on two meals a day. This is always up to each individual.

Listen carefully to your body,
and it will tell you what's going on.

6. Cellular Gases

Understanding the cellular gases is how I formulated the basis for how the body has the potential to heal. This is how it goes!

Carbon dioxide is a normal byproduct of cell metabolism and is eliminated by the respiratory system during exhalation. However, the consumption of mainly processed foods, packaged foods, fractured foods (ex. bran & germ have been removed), foods that have been sprayed with agrochemicals and pesticides or have been treated with hormones, as well as eating foods in the wrong order and combination, results in indigestion and fermentation in the digestive tract, which can create gas pressure throughout the body. Not only can this cause flatulence but this gas created in your body can go from high pressure to low pressure and could move through the mucus membranes of your intestine and into other areas of the body. This could result in a build-up of pressure between the cells and could prevent the release of gas inside the cell.

This process operates according to the principle of simple diffusion. To understand this in more detail, let me quote from *Hole's Human Anatomy and Physiology,* which states:

"Every cell membrane has a barrier that controls which substances enter and leave the cell. Oxygen and nutrient molecules enter through this membrane whereas carbon dioxide leaves through it. These movements involve physical or passive processes such as: diffusion, facilitated diffusion, osmosis and filtration, and physiological (or active) mechanisms such as: active transport, endocytosis and exocytosis. The mechanisms by which substances cross the cell membrane are important for understanding the many aspects of physiology. (This determines the measurement of health of each individual cell and its level of inflammation)

"Diffusion (also called simple diffusion) is the tendency of atoms, molecules, and ions in the liquid or air to move solutions from areas of higher concentration to areas of lower concentration, thus becoming more evenly distributed or diffuse. Diffusion occurs when atoms, molecules and ions are in constant motion. Each particle travels in a separate path along a straight line until it collides with some other particle and bounces off. Then it moves in a new direction till it collides again and changes direction once more. Because collisions are less likely if there are fewer particles, there is a net movement of particles from an area of higher concentration. This difference in concentration is called 'concentration gradient' and atoms, molecules and ions are said to diffuse down a concentration gradient."

This explanation shows beyond a shadow of doubt that gases can move out of the mucus membranes in any part of the human body where there is a higher pressure or a concentration gradient. In other words, gases and fluids through the process of diffusion and osmosis can pass through the mucus membranes from one area of the body to an adjacent area.

In my eight-year study in which I conducted research and did the experiment on myself, I had many experiences that proved to me that the process described above was operating in my body as well as in everyone else's. These experiences enabled me to realize how you could reduce inflammation by simply changing your lifestyle. I have seen people with many different types of pain and illnesses, and the way I approached their condition was to draw on my understanding of the ebb and flow of gases as they relate to their level of inflammation. I realized that I could change the concentration gradient by reducing the gas pressure, thus creating a diffusion equilibrium. The release of these gases occurs mainly by elimination through the bowel, kidneys, lungs and skin.

Though this information about cellular body gases is new to most people, it has been around for a long time. In 1914, for example, Dr. St. Louis Estes wrote in *Back to Nature and a Long Life:* "Gas in the stomach and in the bowels is a chronic disorder characteristic of the reaction of cooked foods. The organs of the body are thwarted in their functions, displaced, prolapsed and diseased through accumulations of these gases which are generated by putrefying foods."

Dr St. Louis Estes also wrote, "Some of the consequences of excess gas are nervousness, headaches, stagnant circulation, cramps, sluggish mentality, dull perceptions, acute indigestion, and numerous aches and pains. The nervous system can become depleted to such an extent that weakness, loss of memory, vertigo, eye troubles, depression, hysteria and even paralysis ensue. Sometimes the pressure is so intense that a large blood vessel gives way. Heart palpitations are also very often caused by intestinal gases. Gas is also an important contributory cause of pyorrhea (teeth and gum problems)."

I have experienced in my personal life, and with my clients who have followed my Intermediate Level Lifestyle, successful results that verify these principles. I have gained a keener awareness of what constitutes a healthy lifestyle by applying the concepts of simple diffusion and cellular gas biology and physiology, which have truly led to a revolution in how I look at the body.

The principle of intercellular gas pressure also explains why it is not a good idea to switch dietary lifestyles. Let's look at a person following the standard American diet, who makes changes to a very healthy diet, such as the Intermediate Level lifestyle, which is a lifestyle that would actually alter a person's chemistry. The improvement in their chemistry and health could be so dramatic that if they went back to the standard American diet too quickly the impact could potentially be detrimental. Their level of cellular gases would be higher because they did not take enough time to readjust to their previous original dietary routine.

This is why we must understand that our life as individuals is a constant process of adaption or re-adaptation that gradually takes place over a period of years. (This is why this requires a commitment for your lifetime) What this means is that, when you go from having a very healthy lifestyle over a period of time and then return too quickly to an unhealthy diet, it could be more destructive than eating a consistently unhealthy diet. Although an unhealthy diet will get you sooner or later down the road, bouncing in and out of different lifestyles is definitely not a good idea!

Remember, one of the major keys in a successful lifestyle change is to choose your parameters and stay within your chosen chemistry. Consistency is where the body will achieve its greatest results and your most thankful rewards.

CHEWING FOOD

Any kind of food will produce gas in the stomach and the bowels if it is not properly masticated (chewed up to a puree or paste). Cooked foods have a natural predisposition to cause gas because they are de-mineralized and devitalized. So the body is unable to absorb or eliminate them efficiently. Also, accumulations of undigested and fermented food can lie in the bowels for extended periods. Over time, they become hardened and as new accumulations are added to the already toxic mass they can decompose and generate more gas increases the pressure in cells. This can be a constant cycle.

Raw foods, because they are alive and vital, do not ferment as readily as cooked foods, but *all* foods do cause gas unless they are **thoroughly masticated**. Solid foods should be ground to the consistency of cream and thoroughly salivated before they are swallowed. The stomach cannot perform the functions of the teeth; if the food is swallowed in chunks the stomach is absolutely incapable of dissolving it, and so only a tiny portion can be absorbed. The result is that undigested chunks of food lie in the stomach, inert and heavy, and fermentation begins shortly thereafter, followed by flatulence, discomfort, indigestion, infrequent bowel movements and often intense gas pain. This will build up gas pressure in the cells, systemically.

Many people eat hearty meals that make them feel uncomfortably full for a while, but within two or three hours they complain of being hungry again. Most times this is not true hunger and it's a mistake to believe that gas, gurgling sounds, bowel discomfort and fermentation in the GI tract or stomach is hunger. This is primarily due to the deficiency of the nutritive value of the foods and secondly to imperfect mastication and overeating. This burdens and drives your body to increase aging process. So if you don't grind/chew/blend the foods to the consistency suitable for assimilation, the stomach puts pressure upon the nerves to absorb enough to satisfy important functions temporarily; but soon more food is required.

This irritation of the stomach is often mistaken for hunger. A stomach overloaded or under-nourished becomes tender and sensitive, and the over functioned and diseased nerves are constantly disturbed. In addition to limiting gas production, proper chewing of foods helps extract nutrients. All foods contain minerals, vitamins and amino acids which are part of their companion nutrient composition. When the foods are crushed with the teeth in the process of mastication, the cells are broken up and these companion nutrients are liberated.

Because of the highly-nutritious properties of raw foods and freshly prepared foods, eaten in their most original, natural state, none of the companion nutrients are lost, so the greatest care should be exercised by those living a raw-food lifestyle. Raw foods have enormous power and are capable of causing great digestive disturbance unless they are thoroughly ground to a creamy consistency with the teeth. Mastication stimulates the salivary glands and causes them to release their secretions, which are essential for optimal digestion and assimilation. The longer the food is chewed the more thoroughly it becomes salivated. This is a daily practice of Your Healthy Journey!

7. Cleansing & Detoxification

When you start changing your diet from lower quality processed foods to higher quality organic plant- based foods, the body must go through phases of chemical adjustments that arise from the elimination of waste products within the cells (toxic endogenous cellular materials). For example, when the use of a stimulant such as coffee, tea, or chocolate is suddenly stopped, headaches may be common while the caffeine and associated theobromine endotoxins are removed from the cells and discarded by the body into the bloodstream during its many circulatory cycles. The endotoxins then exit the body via the intestines, kidneys, lungs and the skin. During this process, detoxification symptoms (aches and pains) may occur and there may also be a feeling of mental or muscular tiredness when the body is deprived of stimulants. This lifestyle change—the elimination of stimulating drinks—in turn produces a slower heart rate that causes a reduction of activity level which you may perceive as an energy letdown. During these periods of chemical adjustment, when the body goes through the process of adaptation, you should **Rest**. Usually within three days the detox symptoms will fade and you will feel stronger as a result of the physical recuperation that follows this adaptation.

Another example is leaving out processed products and replacing them with real, clean, fresh foods. Processed foods are subjected to chemical treatment, additives, artificial spices, preservatives, commercial salt and other harmful alterations that tend to cause unhealthy levels of stimulation to the body. Also, the over consumption of concentrated protein from animal products—meat, chicken, or fish— is more stimulating than less concentrated protein from beans (cooked or sprouted), nuts or seeds. Consequently, a reduction in your consumption of animal protein in exchange for less concentrated plant-based protein produces a slower heart rate which registers as relaxation and possible muscular and mental fatigue.

This relaxation phase may last from three to ten days or slightly longer. It is then followed by an increase in strength and a feeling of greater well-being. This transitional bodily change is an expression of the body's skill at cleaning up on a cellular level. You become more energy efficient each and every time this happens, which is then registered as strength and well-being. **Bravo!**

VARIETIES OF TOXINS

What specifically are some of the toxins that build up inside us, and where do they come from? How do we get rid of them? What symptoms can we expect when they start to leave the body? Here are some of the major culprits:

> **Drugs.** Medicinal or recreational drugs, in practice have to be very powerful in order to overcome the

body's natural immune defense system. When such drugs are taken, they must be either eliminated from the body or stored within the cells and eliminated later.

Every drug that is consumed, whether legal or illegal, leaves its mark upon the body. Old drugs that were taken even many years ago will reappear in the bloodstream as they leave the fat cells of the organs. Drug elimination may express itself in a series of rashes as the toxins leave the body through the skin. If you have any doubt what is happening, please consult with a healthcare provider.

Although the detoxification process can be lengthy and does occur at different times during your lifetime, the process can be accelerated by fasting on vegetable juices and leading a lifestyle that includes large amounts of fresh fruits and vegetables.

Caffeine & Nicotine. Heavy smokers or coffee drinkers may experience nervous irritability and emotional outbreaks when they are detoxifying. Nicotine and caffeine damage the nervous system and upset the vascular system, so symptoms such as headaches, edginess, and extreme lassitude may be expected.

Salt & other condiments. Condiments are taken only to stimulate taste and few of them can be used by the body efficiently, which as a result the body has to store them in the cells. (Some unrefined salts and spices, have a benefit in moderation on the body, but should not be overdone). In Mexico, corpses have been found in the deserts that were untouched by buzzards and hyenas because these people had eaten such large quantities of hot peppers all their lives that their skin was actually too spicy for the scavengers to eat.

When you discontinue the use of condiments, the body begins the process of elimination and old cellular deposits exit through the skin and kidneys. Sometimes the elimination is so intense that a person may have a continual salty taste in the mouth for days. The skin may become crusted with salt or it may smell of the particular condiment that is being eliminated, such as onions, peppers, or vinegar. Salt elimination may also cause a temporary rise in blood pressure, which then renormalizes itself and eventually descends below the average norm.

White sugar. Eliminating sugar from the life may make a person feel slightly nervous and hyperactive until the energy levels adjust to the change. Reformed sugar addicts may feel periods of unaccountable depression as their blood sugar level tries to right itself. Getting off the sugar rollercoaster, with its rapid rises and falls in blood sugar levels, is easier to do when you eat raw foods. Your Healthy Journey re-normalizes blood sugar levels and promotes emotional tranquility.

Heavy metals. Almost everyone is poisoned by heavy metal deposits in the body because of the environment all around us from manufacturing. Lead can enter the body through auto and factory exhaust, paints, and canned foods. Aluminum may come from preparing or storing food in aluminum containers and Arsenic is present on sprayed foods.

Lead, aluminum, copper, and arsenic collect in organs throughout the body and since these metals are heavy, they tend to remain in the body until a cleansing lifestyle or fast is followed. As these metals are eliminated headaches and general achiness throughout the body may occur. The gums may hurt and the kidneys may throb as these metals leave the organs and bones. Occasionally, you can actually taste the metal that is being eliminated. Lead especially often leaves a metallic taste on the tongue when it is leaving the body. As you eliminate these metals, bear the uncomfortable body aches and realize that they are leaving your body. Thank goodness!

Acidity. Cooked and processed foods create an acid condition in the body. When they are eliminated, (left out) the body tries to reestablish its naturally healthy, alkaline condition. As the acid condition of the body changes to one of alkalinity, symptoms may arise that may be confusing. A sour, disagreeable odor may be emitted from the body as the acids leave or are neutralized. Hair may fall out and the breath may turn fowl. Urine may be very dark and sharp; there also may be a bitter taste in the mouth and fatigue and weakness of the arms and legs may occur.

Many people, if they are reducing or giving up animal products, confuse this weakness with protein deficiency. Instead, this weakness has resulted from an over consumption of too many acid-forming foods from your past. The majority of acid–forming foods is the processed foods and is inventoried in the What You Leave Out List. The body's energies are mainly directed toward neutralizing these old toxins, so you may feel weak for a temporary period; but once the toxins are taken care of and an alkaline condition is reestablished, the strength returns to the limbs. The discomfort of an over-acid body can be quickly overcome by a high alkaline lifestyle.

This doesn't mean that you have to eliminate all acid forming foods from Your Healthy Journey. The trick is to eat alkalinizing foods first – juices, salad – which will neutralize the effect of the moderate amounts of acid foods. For example, if you eat a salad and then follow it with a moderate quantity of grass-fed, organic meat, the harm to your body will be minimal or non-existent. Moreover, if you are diligent about keeping up your water and vegetable juice intake, that will remove the toxins from your system. Also the body's chemistry and homeostasis are the main factors in creating the right PH in the blood (7.35-7.45) and the right acid/alkaline balance. When your lifestyle is a predominately plant-based, raw food lifestyle, you are giving your body the potential to decrease the possibility of chronic breakdown and thrive optimally throughout your life.

SPECIFIC INDICATORS

Most people who change their existing diet and improve their health through a lifestyle change may experience one or more of the indicators described below. This all depends upon your past health, because these indicators may be mild or intense, short-term or long-term, temporary or recurrent. So as you improve and stay on Your Healthy Journey, all symptoms will gradually disappear over time. But remember that during detoxification, if you halt any symptoms with any other stimulating foods or activities, they will only reappear later with greater intensity.

Almost all symptoms experienced during a lifestyle change are due to the body's efforts to detoxify as rapidly as possible. You can help in this process by skipping a few solid food meals, drinking fresh vegetable juices, light eating and getting plenty of rest. Be sure you get all the sleep you need and try to avoid stressful situations. Moderate exercise, when appropriate may be beneficial if the time is right. Sunshine, fresh air and freedom from stress are vital while detoxing.

Above all else, cultivate a positive attitude about what you are doing and give yourself as much peace and privacy as possible. You may feel that you are punishing yourself or that you are making great sacrifices but you 're really recovering your health and there can be no greater reward than that. Realize that your sincere efforts will give you a level of quality health exceeding your wildest dreams. Do not dwell upon your temporary discomforts; instead, indulge in positive activity, helping others that may be interested. All symptoms will pass in time. The intensity you feel today will be just a decreased memory tomorrow. Remember the discomforts you endure now mean an absence of suffering later. You will have much to be thankful for as you continue on Your Healthy Journey.

Headaches. If you are told by your physician that there is nothing organically wrong with you then a headache is the body's expression of toxicity. As you detoxify, the toxic load in the body can start to increase so fast that poisons circulating in the blood stream cause irritation to the brain and nerves. To obtain some relief, lie down and rest with a cool, damp cloth across the eyes and forehead. Juice fasting may also help, have someone massage your neck and temples and avoid all stress at this time.

Upset stomach and diarrhea. When food is not being digested properly or is passing right through your body, then it is time to stop all food intake. This is your body's way of telling you it doesn't require any nourishment at this time, but instead is busy housecleaning. Be careful of your food combinations and avoid heavy, concentrated foods. Rest, abstinence from food for a period of time, and consumption of vegetable juices are your best options.

Constipation. A lifestyle change may occasionally bring up constipation. Brisk walking of at least one mile a day will help end this problem. Eating/chewing raw foods high in water content and fiber will also eventually remedy this condition. So drink your vegetable juices before meals and as you stay consistent with the lifestyle change, constipation disappears, and a regular bowel movement returns.

Weight loss. Weight loss may occur in the early stages of this kind of lifestyle. Exercises for muscle growth, such as weight lifting, martial arts, Pilates, and swimming, will help rebuild the body with lean, muscular tissue when the time is right . Be sure that your lifestyle includes a proper balance between the water plump foods and concentrated foods so you will create the proper balance to normalize your body weight. When your body starts to renormalize, you can expect to lose any excess weight that your body is retaining and you will stabilize at a healthy and vibrant body weight.

A word of warning: If you or someone you know has any kind of eating disorder, you should seek professional advice before embarking on a mostly raw food lifestyle or any kind of lifestyle change. For example, an anorexic who counts calories, eats only greens, and indulges in a lot of exercise will cannibalize their own body for fuel, which creates a life-threatening situation. A mostly raw, plant-based lifestyle done correctly by a an emotionally and psychologically stable person is healthy and is not in itself dangerous—on the contrary for over 50 years I have seen many people where it is lifesaving—but like anything else that's beneficial, it can be done incorrectly, misused and become harmful.

WATER

Concerning the type of water you should drink, after experimenting for over 50 years by drinking all types of water, I've come to the conclusion beyond a shadow of a doubt that ionized water is essential for good health. The negative ions and antioxidant and alkaline quality of ionized water is far superior because the minerals in water are electrical conductors. These colloidal minerals help communicate the electrical charge between cells.

You should drink a few glasses of water in the morning, to set yourself up for the day. The general rule is that your daily consumption should be ½ your body weight in fluid ounces of water. This is not a hard and fast rule; there are special circumstances according to your daily activities, based on your lifestyle and athletic endeavors. It stands to reason if a person was eating a diet high in protein, starches and processed food they would have to drink more water than a person that was eating a water plump plant-based lifestyle with lots of fruits and vegetables. We should remember that water is a solvent and transport medium which could actually be more important mechanically than food. You can survive much longer without food than you can without water. If you are on a mostly raw, whole food lifestyle and drink several glasses of vegetable juices a day, you need less water than the recommended amount.

8. Sleep, Rest, & Exercise

When I was a young man and was working out, power weighting I ate a high protein diet. I always needed a lot of sleep and in fact I had to take naps, but now, at this point in my life, (born 1929) I only need three to four hours of sleep a night.

How many hours of sleep a person needs depends on the condition of their blood, which is dependent on the food they eat. When you are sleeping, your blood goes into the process of dialysis; it's cleaning up on a cellular level and your going through anabolism. If your diet is terrible, you might need 12 hours of sleep. Also, the amount of energy that you expend on digestion and assimilation from breaking down food influences the amount of sleep you require.

If you chew your food, eat only to satisfaction, food combine, consume plant-based foods, and eat a high percentage of raw plant foods, you will expend far less energy than someone on the standard American diet. On the other hand, if you are going through deep biological healing, even on a good diet you'll need as much sleep as you can get—as much as 15 hours.

Getting enough rest is very important. Most people do not get enough rest because they are stimulating themselves with food and activities. Excessive tension in your life also makes you tired. So think about introducing some relaxation techniques into your routine—if you look around, you'll find many to choose from; deep breathing, meditation, prayer and good friends that listen.

When you're following the raw food lifestyle, correctly you will have an abundance of vitality and energy, and you will want to go out and exercise. If you do not have that strong desire to use your body, there is something you're missing and you need to find out what it is.

On raw foods, you will see exercise in a new light. Consider how wild animals use their bodies: they are constantly roaming; they do not have a regular exercise program, and yet they are always fit. The same will be true for you—you will be automatically fit. You can have a regular exercise routine, if that is better for your lifestyle but you can also just go out and work out very easily without any training.

9. Individual Differences

There are individual differences with cultures, groups and geographic locations. Let's say you are from an Eastern European background in which there has been a tradition of heavy meat consumption for five or six generations. This genetic aspect becomes part of your tissue quality, which means, if you wanted to leave out meat from your lifestyle, it would have to be a gradual transition.

Your geographic region and climate are also important. If you were an Eskimo in the North Pole, and only ate raw fish and seal, you couldn't survive on pineapples, mangos and watermelons, because those water-plump foods don't hold enough resistance. They are not dense enough to maintain your basal metabolism and keep you warm. On the other hand, if you live down near the equator, you don't want to subsist on pork chops or sausage, because heavy foods of that kind will make you constantly sweaty, weak, and sleepy. In this environment, you should eat more water-plump fruits and vegetables, because you don't need dense foods in order to maintain your basal metabolism.

That's why certain branches of oriental medicine tell people to eat foods that are grown in their environment because, given the ambient temperature, they'll be more compatible with their chemistry.

10. Eat to Live

Eating food or drinking liquids is not a recreational activity; it should be used for the purpose it's supposed to serve. Of course, eating is a celebration of life and sharing fellowship with friends and family is wonderful. There are also special occasions when food is very important. But unfortunately in our society we take it to an extreme. Everything now revolves around food. It's a continuous ongoing event, like an Olympic event to see who can eat the most and enjoy as many different tastes in the same meal as possible.

Sometimes healthy eaters can become obsessed in a different way. While a healthy lifestyle is important, you don't want to become neurotic about it. Some people on a raw food lifestyle go off the deep end and all they can think about is their next meal. Some may decide that to achieve maximum health they have to divorce the wife, abandon the kids, move to a remote island and live off coconuts and spring water. But that is not my idea of a healthy lifestyle. Food is just fuel so you can live a full and healthy life. There are a lot of magnificent things out there, besides food—fresh air, a beautiful place that you enjoy in the country, music, art, family, and friends.

I used to speak to people about food and lifestyle every day, seven days a week, sometimes from ten to twelve hours a day. This was a good experience and this helped me understand a lot about the human body. But it gets to be too much when somebody only wants to talk about food. For example: I'm trying to enjoy a wedding reception and someone approaches me and just wants to talk about food. I am a polite person but I had to excuse myself from this conversation. Sometimes it's just too much. It's best to not force yourself on someone when they are not receptive or the occasion is not suitable. There's a right time and a place for everything.

I also socialize with people that eat the worst diets in the world and they are fantastic friends. We have other interests in common—sports, music, art, books, and just enjoying ourselves. The other night a few of us spent some time together till two o'clock in the morning; we had a lot of fun just kicking things around because we respect each other decisions.

So, my recommendation is: eat in order to live, but don't live in order to eat!

11. Mind, Body, Spirit

I've spoken a lot about living a lifestyle and how it is important, and now I'd like to include as part of Your Healthy Journey something else that needs to be considered, which is more important than the physical: namely, the spiritual inward life.

Without this spiritual direction, we are likely to succumb to all the wrong desires and vices of the flesh in the world, and slip into disease and degradation, and not even be aware of it.

As your body gets better and your blood becomes purer, what happens is that the awareness of your mind opens up. To help facilitate this, eat a dominant amount of raw foods as possible, practice unconditional love, and look to God for your inner direction. As you progress you will get free of the spiritual, moral, and physical dependence the world imposes on you. You will realize your divine inheritance, which is a gift from God, and you will understand how to make this a better world.

I have noticed that living a raw food lifestyle has led me to the depth and height of my mental and spiritual capacity. Humans only use 8 to 12 percent of their conscious brain.

The purer your blood is, the better your brain is going to work. So when you commit to Your Healthy Journey, your mental sharpness and spiritual clarity become elevated. You don't need to go to India and start chanting and meditating all day in a temple in order to raise your consciousness. It just will happen, if you are aware of it!

The condition of the human body, is spiritually and vibrationally induced, electrically and chemically empowered, and biologically and genetically carried out. What this means is that the spiritual dimension is primary foundation. As I have frequently observed, "We are spiritual beings having a physical experience", not the other way round.

When you put the whole package together, there is an outside source whose purpose is to give you inner direction in your life, if you allow it. Then you will understand that the work is more about spirituality than food. I really don't think about food very much, and I believe that's one of the keys to my success. My spiritual life and my complete commitment to my faith in God, I believe, empowered me to accomplish just about anything. Faith is one of the most powerful forces on earth and can change not only people but also the world.

You also have to consider everything as a whole. It's a total lifestyle change. For example, if you think negative thoughts all the time and you're full of hatred, animosity, fear, and doubt, this is going to have an effect on your body's chemistry and physiology. Once you realize that you can actually change who you are and what you're doing, you are then empowered to overcome things that most people assume can never be changed. Many of us are naysayers—you can't do this or you can't do that—but I don't buy into that philosophy. I believe that if you are committed, obtain the right information, strive for higher ideals, don't settle for mediocrity, keep searching, and remain committed to a lifestyle program, you will evolve into the best of who you are in every respect—physically, emotionally, psychologically, and spiritually.

Can a mere lifestyle change have an impact not only on the mind and body but also on the spirit? Absolutely Yes! To what degree? It depends on your commitment. You can always rationalize or find a reason not to change your lifestyle but this will make your problems just persist. Your hesitation tells you that you really don't want to change. The initial step in growth is to make the commitment to strive to be a better person. You want to commit your life to being not only a blessing to yourself but an example to others—demonstrating to them what you really can accomplish. The sky's the limit in this regard; you are only limited by your own abstract thinking. If you change this abstract thinking to a tangible commitment, you can be taken to a level of health, well-being, positive thinking, good habits, and happiness beyond anything you can currently imagine.

"WHAT YOU LEAVE OUT IS KEY"

PART II
The Plan

1. Setting Lifetime Parameters

Eating Guidelines: It's **What You Leave Out** then it's **What You Put In.** The system really works, but you have to draw on deep reserves of determination, awareness, and commitment in order to achieve your goal of having a healthier life. Your part is to understand that this process of a lifestyle change is for your whole lifetime, which involves personal accountability and responsibility. Every life event shows you your ability to learn and grow from this experience. Remember, with every new experience at first you don't know what you don't know. Then you go through the journey offered by that experience, and by the end you do know. So open your mind and heart in order to get ready to learn, and let's go on Your Healthy Journey.

The most important aspect of setting your parameters is deciding what processed foods and stimulating drinks you will drop from the "Leave Out" list. What items are you willing to leave out of your lifestyle forever, without being overwhelmed? What can you commit to that will be workable for you in everyday life? Some heroic people may simply go ahead and leave it all out. I do not doubt this can be done, and the results would be marvelous. But the more practical path for setting realistic parameters will be constructed over your whole life, where your body is showing you that the more you leave out, the more efficient you become. These are your healing pathways working for you.

I suggest when you're establishing new parameters that you really know what you can stick to, rather than allowing yourself to be carried away by the initial enthusiasm that will not stand the test of time. As I mentioned in the Principles, the **worst** thing you can do to your body is to force it to change its chemistry and make it bounce back. This is what happens when you swing in and out of your parameters.

So when you stop eating or drinking items from the "Leave Out" list, a reciprocal action of healing/detox/ cleansing occurs in the body. Your physical body which does not recognize what you eat or drink as foods but as chemicals that create interactions. The body either utilizes it for fuel, storage or elimination. If you live in an industrialized country, your body has probably become inundated by the over-consumption of processed foods. When it can no longer eliminate the huge amount of chemical residues contained in these foods, it will deposit them as chemical waste/storage in the cells. This will effect your genetic expression, where the epigenetic switches of every cell are turned on or off, which will affect various functions within your body.

The good news is that you get healthier over time and ultimately have the potential to reverse the damage you may have unintentionally done to yourself, if you adjust yourself to the following lifestyle changes:

- **80% plant-based** (fruits, vegetables, nuts, seeds, sprouts) and **20 % protein-based** (whole grains, legumes, grass fed beef, free range chicken) foods instead of a high protein or fat-based approach.

- **Real Freshly Prepared Foods** instead of processed foods.

- **Raw organic fruits, vegetables, seeds, nuts, and sprouts** instead of canned and conventional items.

- **Grass fed beef and organic chicken** instead of commercial beef or chicken.

- **A moderate amount of whole grains, legumes, or a small amount of animal protein if necessary in the right combinations** instead of improper food combining.

- **Three solid food meals a day only,** no snacking between or after meals (letting your stomach empty between meals helps the body detoxify, when you keep it full all day by glazing on solid food & snacks, this stops the detox/cleansing process).

- **Eating solid foods after 9am & 3- 4 hours before bed** instead of eating too early in the morning or too late at night.

In order to set your parameters you need to determine what the following ratios will be:

- *Raw/uncooked portions to* cooked choices
- *Organic* to conventional foods
- *Plant-based* to animal-based foods

- *Vegetables* to animal protein
- *Vegetables* to fruits
- *Vegetable greens* to fats
- *Monosaturated* to saturated fats
- *Low glycemic* to high glycemic fruits
- *Less concentrated proteins* (seeds and nuts) to high Concentrated proteins (beef, chicken, turkey, and fish)

Whether you want to eat a vegan lifestyle (plant based, fruits, vegetables, nuts, seeds & sprouts) or a lifestyle that's a combination of plant and animal foods, parameters can be created so you can enjoy a healthy lifestyle. This is where the First Foundation of **what you leave out** becomes very important. When you commit to leaving out everything that is harmful to your body, it will adjust to the change in chemistry and take the necessary action to re-establish homeostasis. To facilitate this process, you require an adequate supply of all the essential nutrients from **what you put in**. This is one of the keys to your longevity.

So your first task is to build your foundation by deciding what you're going to commit to leave out and what you're going to leave in. The whole secret to following and adjusting to a healthy lifestyle is to create workable parameters and then live within them, regardless of what others may think or say. Living this way may not be popular and does have social ramifications, but it's truely right for the body when you're looking for quality health and longevity.

2. Juices and Salads

Meals should begin with a water-plump base of delicious vegetables juices and delightful salads. The reason for starting your meals with high water-content food combinations in the form of fresh juices and salads is that water is a solvent and a transport medium. This aids many other functions such as kidney support, maintaining a proper body temperature, hydration, proper elimination and cleansing from the bowels.

Juices and salads should be made with fresh plant-based foods on a daily basis—organic produce is preferred when available. Vegetables juices should be consumed for all three meals each day, if possible. There are juice recipes and proportions described in this book . There are also plenty of businesses that prepare these juices but the most effective way is to buy a juicer yourself. Juicers that range from the least to most expensive include: Breville, Omega and Norwalk. One of my favorite juices is apple, celery and a variety of greens.

In this water-plump approach, the juices should be consumed first and then be followed up by a large salad. A raw vegetable juice requires less amount of time and energy to digest and assimilate than a salad, so follow the order. This is a very important process to understand.

Your salad should have a high percentage of greens with a five to seven vegetable combination included. The ingredients of the salad should be cut into small pieces so it's easier to chew and digest. The salad dressing should also be made fresh. The ingredients can include extra-virgin olive oil, hemp oil, or flax oil, with lemon or raw apple cider vinegar and a small portion of fresh herbs or nut butters can be added as a slight accent of flavor.

If you have cooked food portions with your meal which is fine, make sure you eat it after you eat the dominant raw food portions first. (Eating the alkaline then the acid) The uncooked foods are alkaline and, when eaten first in the same meal, serve to balance chemically the cooked foods, which are acidic.

3. Balancing The Scale

The balancing scale is the efficiency and exchanges of whole foods that requires greater or lesser outputs of energy/time for their digestion and assimilation. This determines your parameters!

ENERGY AND TIME

When we are following parameters, we start by qualifying foods. This classification of foods is determined by what requires the most or least amount of energy and time to digest and assimilate. As we introduce foods that come closest to their natural, original state (*Real, Fresh Foods*, freshly prepared as dominantly raw and moderately cooked portions to meals), in which the quality/quantity, food combinations, and eating sequence are balanced, we enter the path that leads to health and Your Healthy Journey.

When you consider the energy efficiency, time factoring of foods and how it bears and endures on your body, *Real, Fresh Foods* are the way to go compared with processed foods. Remember, *Real, Fresh Foods* that are organic are preferred if available. These are complete whole foods because looking at the labels on packaged processed foods, do you recognize any wholesome ingredients? How many chemical ingredients are listed? All these factors are associated with the time it takes and the energy your body expends to utilize these chemical variables. The fewer artificial ingredients, the better.

Real, Fresh Foods are wholesome foods; that start whole and are not broken apart from their companion nutrients. Fruits, vegetables, seeds, nuts, sprouts or whole grains serve as examples. When I use the word wholesome you have to realize that most of the food people are eating is not *Real, Fresh Foods.* It is a highly processed food, which has been perverted from its original state and is no longer viewed by the body's biochemistry as an original food. Most packaged and processed foods are broken up, rearranged and altered with added chemicals and preservatives. They are not going to have the same beneficial effects for quality and longevity as wholesome foods. It all depends on how the liver reacts!

THE LIVER

The liver is a very important organ that performs over 500 different functions and has to deal with these rearranged and altered chemicals. The main function is that of a filter. The liver has to work harder and spend more time to deal with foods (processed) that are not in their original state. Foods that are in their original state—*Real Fresh Foods*— require no struggle or wear or tear on the body because of the synchronicity of their companion nutrients that are left intact which are easily broken down.

Depending on the quantity of processed foods you consume and your genetic predisposition, you can finally get to a point where your liver will no longer be able to deal with the insult. Then chemical residues will be stored somewhere else in your body—it could be anywhere in your cells—and this will hinder your body's ability to function at its peak performance. So when you live a life of processed and concentrated foods, this will cause an intoxicating exogenous effect on the human body. This precursor is the loss of health, life, and optimal well being.

So all food should be wholesome: either fresh in its raw or natural state, or slightly heated and as close to nature as it was originally given to us. This will give you a much greater chance of staying within your parameters where we can maintain a high quality of life to an advanced age for a long, long time.

THE PROTEIN SCALE

If a person exchanges a protein rich (concentrated) food such as pork with beef, the beef will be the lesser of the two due to its easier digestibility and its lower saturated fat content. When beef is exchanged for chicken and chicken exchanged for fish, this opens another progression revealing greater efficiency and understanding. The next level will be to exchange fish for lima beans, lentils or chickpeas and then lima beans, lentils or chickpeas for nuts and seeds. As you can see the scale from beef to nuts represents increasingly easier levels of digestibility, in less time and increases your reserves of energy in storage. When you use less energy output you will slow down the aging process.

THE CARBOHYDRATE SCALE

Whole grains are classified as complex carbohydrates. This is the most efficient way to utilize glucose for health and longevity. This chemical complex is a sugar with two or more molecules. Complex carbohydrates are more easily absorbed than animal protein and more slowly absorbed than simple sugars. As the carbohydrates are absorbed, they are gradually broken down into glucose. This chemical breakdown facilitates the process of assimilation for all energy as fuel in the body. Carbohydrates are scaled in three ways: from more to less energy/time outputs, from most acidic to most alkaline, and from more glutinous to non-glutinous (the amount of gluten they contain).

Gluten is a sticky protein present in some grains, and it is classified as starch. Gluten is hard to digest, which can lead to congestion in the body. There is usually a high degree of inflammation associated with it, which is a good reason to seek out less starchy, non-glutinous grains. Leaving out wheat, oats, barley and rye which contain gluten, and exchanging it with brown rice, millet, buckwheat, cornmeal, amaranth, and quinoa is the way to go.

Processed grains have the highest level of gluten and form an acid ash. When you process a grain, you heat it and then remove the bran fiber and the germ nutrients. What remains is starch plus the added chemicals and preservatives. If you exchange the most processed starchy grains—such as white flour products, pastas, white rice, cold or prepared cereals, pretzels, and crackers—with a starchy unprocessed grain such as wheat, oats, barley and rye, the latter would be the better of the two. Starchy grains—wheat, oats, barley and rye—exchanged for brown rice, millet, buckwheat, cornmeal, legumes, amaranth, quinoa, gluten-free bread and brown rice pasta represents a progression to an easier level of digestibility. Exchanging your cooked unprocessed grains for sprouted grains or seeds is even better.

At another level, brown rice, millet, buckwheat, cornmeal, amaranth, quinoa, gluten-free bread and brown rice pasta are exchanged for sweet potato, squash or yams. After that, sweet potatoes, squash or yams are exchanged for carrots, peas and beets—this brings you to the simplest exchange for digestion and assimilation.

Sugar-rich foods which are one molecule and are classified as simple carbohydrates, should be **left out,** because they are loaded with starches, salt, fat and refined sugars which may give you a burst of energy in the short run but it only speeds up the aging process in the long run.

FATS

Fats are qualified in two categories as saturated or unsaturated. Saturated fats are associated products from animals. They harden at room temperature, are a factor in elevating your cholesterol and clog arteries. Unsaturated fats, which are plant fats, include olive, hemp, flaxseed, nut and seed oils, and nut and seed butters. These oils do not harden at room temperature and are best when cold pressed. The simple exchange is to replace saturated with unsaturated oils. This is an ideal way of getting your essential fats and we all need our **essential fats.**

VEGETABLES

Mineral-rich vegetable foods are the basis for this water plump, plant-based approach. They should be eaten at every meal. They are a secondary source of energy, sun being the primary. All green leafy vegetables are loaded with more minerals than vitamins, even though they do contain the latter. The lists of mineral-rich vegetable foods are: Leafy Greens, Lettuces, Spinach, Romaine, Chicory, Kale, Boston

Bibb, Endive, Collards, Escarole, Arugula, Red Tip, Green Curley, Mesclun, Fennel, Watercress, Chard, Barley and Alfalfa Grasses. Salad Ingredients: Cucumber, Celery, Red/Yellow or Green Pepper, Tomato (all varieties), Zucchini, Broccoli, Cauliflower, String Beans, Asparagus, Yellow Squash, Cabbage, Okra, Avocado. Sea Vegetables: Dulse, Kelp, Nori, Arame.

FRUITS

Vitamin-rich fruits are another important part of this water-plump approach. They are considered the best source of energy as fuel (glucose) with a high vitamin nutrient value, more so than vegetables. They are rich in plant sugars and are a secondary source of energy, sun being the primary. The list of vitamin-rich fruits includes: Oranges (all varieties), Grapefruits, Lemons, Limes, Coconuts, Grapes, Raisins, Figs, Apricots, Apples (all varieties), Pears, Peaches, Cherries, all Berries, Plums, Bananas, Kiwis, Medjool Dates, Watermelons, Melons, Cantaloupe, Crenshaw, Honeydew, Papayas, Mangoes, and Pineapples. Avocados and Peppers are also classified botanically as fruits but I consider these two in the vegetable category.

Concerning fruit, it is important to consider the glycemic Index which is how sugars are assimilated into the body. As a general rule, berries, cherries, grapefruit and mangoes are low on the scale, while bananas and dried fruits are high. Although there is a glycemic scale associated with fruit, it should be understood that the companion nutrients from the fiber and the minerals and vitamins inside stabilize the sugars so insulin levels are balanced in the bloodstream. Fructose extracted from fruit and any other refined sugars do not have the same balanced effect in the body. Leave them out!

4. Core Products & Living Foods

When someone changes their lifestyle, eats a high proportion of raw foods, does it in the correct and balanced manner and get all the nutrients they need, they should not require a lot of supplements. Some experts recommend mega doses of of vitamins/minerals. My experience over the years has been that if you live a good nutritional lifestyle it is not necessary.

Although, if you are a strict vegetarian, it's a good idea to evaluate to see if you need vitamin B12. If you're not a vegetarian and you're below four hundred pico-grams, you could be symptomatic. Also, if you are living above the fortieth parallel level—in New York City or Alaska, for example—and you're not getting much sunshine, you need to be aware of the potential for a vitamin D deficiency.

In my practice, I evaluate every person as an individual, from their own lifestyle, physiology, and environment, then I suggest what they really need. I then find the cleanest, purest form of a supplement/product, as close to a natural food as possible, in low dosages so the body doesn't interpret it as a high stimulant chemical.

There are various products that are considered to be supplements, which are actually not supplements at all. Enzymes, probiotics, super-green foods (such as chlorella, spirulina, barley, alfalfa, wheat grass juice, E-3Live and bluegreen algae) are food products and a powerful addition to a lifestyle change. I don't consider them to be stimulating supplements because they are live foods, which can be extremely beneficial because they work with your body for better functionality and an easier transition through detox/elimination phases. So once you have made your commitment to the lifestyle of Your Healthy Journey there are four categories of Core Products and Living Foods that I strongly suggest that work as an adjunct with the whole human body, systemically, Enzymes, Probiotics and Super Greenfoods which can be found at the website. (www.anydoubtleaveitout.com)

ENZYMES

Enzymes participate in every chemical reaction and are associated with every system function in every cell in the body. There are 3000 metabolic enzyme actions that are known. Any condition/inflammation that you are experiencing requires the work of these enzymes, which are the backbone of your immune and organ systems.

Besides your enzyme systems being burdened by poor dietary lifestyle choices, when you eat cooked foods enzymes are destroyed by heat. Then enzymes are taken from the body's supply to digest the food. This causes your store of enzymes to become over utilized and depleted over time, which can lead to many health problems. On the other hand, living the lifestyle of Your Healthy Journey helps maintain your supply of enzymes and spares the energy overuse conversion. Most of us have been eating cooked foods all our lives and as a result our enzyme bank has become bankrupt and inefficient. For example, the average person will typically will expend 60%-70% energy on eating a meal. We should only be expending 10%-15%. All of this requires enzymes. This in turn takes away the functionality from some other system in the body. Remember metabolic enzymes are catalyst proteins and are involved in every function in the body; without enzymes we would not exist.

SYSTEMIC ENZYMES

Systemic enzymes (plant-based) are suggested so that you can spare the conversion and usage from your existing enzyme pool and help you deal with the body's normal inflammatory and healing process. Their action is similar in nature to your existing metabolic enzyme system. Sparing this conversion lets your natural enzyme supply stay intact because it does require energy by the body to utilize metabolic enzymes, so taking systemic enzymes helps the body have better functional efficiency. This is an energy- saver and an important process in the body's remedial healing capabilities.

Systemic enzymes should be taken on an empty stomach, 45 minutes before your meals, in between meals, or 2 hours after your meals. It is usually suggested to take them when you wake up and when you go to bed.

DIGESTIVE ENZYMES

Digestive enzymes (plant-based) are utilized for aiding in the digestion of food. When you are taking digestive enzymes with your meals, again you are sparing this conversion that takes place from your natural pool. Digestive enzymes helps reduces the discomfort of incomplete digestion, while actually improving the breakdown of carbohydrates, fats and proteins. Digestive enzymes are specifically designed to break down a broad range of foods into nutrients your body can readily use. They should be effective across a wide pH range throughout the entire digestive tract. This will make you more efficient and is an energy-saver for the body. Digestive enzymes should be taken with your meals.

Keep in mind that enzymes are a raw living food and are based on a water plump plant-based approach for your daily lifestyle.

PROBIOTICS

Probiotics are friendly bacteria that improve our existing intestinal flora and make a vital contribution to our overall health. There are about 100 trillion cells in the body and 1,000 trillion bacteria in the body. So we have to be able live symbiotically within our body with these bacteria because the main activities exist with the 100 trillion bacteria that live in our gastrointestinal tract. Although there are small populations of certain bacteria in the bowel that are very harmful, there needs to be large population of good bacteria in the bowel. These good bacteria take care of proper digestion, help maintain energy and efficiency levels in the body and strengthen the immune system.

Many people today have problems with the gastro-intestinal tract because it is loaded with all kinds of yeast, fungus and molds. All this puts a heavy stress on your immune system. It's like a sewage system, and probiotics clean the system up. We have to be aware that there are many factors, internally and externally, that affect the population of these good bacteria such as: stress levels, illness, infections, drugs, antibiotics, environmental pollution and a poor diet (mainly), to name a few. These factors will affect the population balance of good bacteria, which will impair function in the body because the low levels of harmful bacteria are an energy drainer and create inefficiency.

Good probiotics facilitate bowel elimination, promote regularity, assist in managing cholesterol, alleviate flatulence, bloating, belching, increase the availability of nutrients, fight harmful bacteria, fungi, and viruses, support healthy liver function and help unburden the immune system. Probiotics are a blend of live populations of good bacteria that colonize the whole digestive system.

Although, we can and do obtain intestinal flora from fruits, vegetables, and plant-based foods, which is why I recommend a plant-based approach as the foundation but most people can nullify the effects from the inefficiencies of how they actually live their lifestyle. So taking probiotics as a supplement gives you an edge.

Probiotics are a living food and are based on a water-plump, plant-based lifestyle. They can be taken in the morning, at night, with meals or throughout the course of the day when you have cravings.

SUPER GREENFOODS

BLUE-GREEN ALGAE, E-3 LIVE, WHEATGRASS, BARLEY GRASSES, CHLORELLA, SPIRULINA & ALFALFA

Super greenfoods are fantastic and I use them typically, every day. When I first started on a raw plant food lifestyle it was very simple. There was no Super greenfoods but many years ago when I started doing green powders I really noticed an improvement in my strength and energy level and saw the value of introducing this into a healthy lifestyle. All the varieties of greenfoods have a unique purpose and can be used on Your Healthy Journey. These super foods come in a juice, frozen or powder. The frozen form of E-3Live, which has been researched extensively, is a highly nutrient-dense food and is also a good choice. All these foods contain chlorophyll, amino acids, antioxidants, vitamins, essential fats, minerals, enzymes and probiotics. They are complete raw living foods and are based on a water-plump, plant-based approach for your daily lifestyle. They can be added into your vegetable juice, blended salad or a smoothie.

5. The General Rules

The biological lifestyle for optimum health is Fruits, Vegetables, Nuts, Seeds, and Sprouts (fresh and uncooked) and steamed grains and cooked portions in small quantities. **AVOID:** smoke, exhaust fumes, food additives, artificial colors and flavors, preservatives, plant foods sprayed with pesticides and chemically fertilized—BUT if you use them, wash them well.

Exercise is important to keep well and helps promote cell revitalization. 20 minutes 3 times a week is sufficient but you can do more within reason—Resistance & Stretching Exercise, Rebounding, Yoga, Tai Chi, Pilates, Martial Arts, Walking, Competitive Sports, etc.

Dry brush massaging before shower or bath supports the lymphatic system

Three basic types of food: Concentrated Foods (Proteins—nuts, seeds, animal meats. Carbohydrates—grains, rice, whole rice pasta, beans, potatoes); High Water Content Foods (fruits and vegetables) and Fats (mono and saturated, nuts, seeds, olives).

Protein is the most complex concentrated food and requires the most energy and time to digest and assimilate.

Fruit is the least complex, high water content food and takes the least energy and time to digest and assimilate. It is best eaten in moderation on an empty stomach as a meal in itself. You can have fruit with nuts 30-45 minutes later as a meal option. You can also have fruit as an occasional lunch/dinner option.

For post exercise, a blended fruit smoothie with greens or green powder can be consumed within 30-45 minutes to replace your glycogen. After that you can eat your main meal 2 hours later. If you are going to eat more fruit the same day wait at least 3 hours. Fruit is best at your morning meal.

Glucose (sugar) is the brain's only and most efficient food because it cannot burn protein or fat as an energy source.

Eating correct food combinations (at proper times, for example 3-4 hours before bedtime) are essential for effective digestion and assimilation that leads to optimum quality health, energy, and state of well being.

All sugars, including Fruits, have been classified as a carbohydrate by science, but fruit by itself is a separate category that exists as a whole sugar. This confusing norm of classifying a fruit as a carbohydrate has led to the consumption of fruit as a poor combination with protein or with other carbohydrates in the same meal. This leads to digestive difficulties because this poor combination requires more digestive energy and should be avoided. (IT'S WHAT YOU LEFT OUT)

In the digestive system, the processes for breaking down proteins, carbohydrates and fruits are entirely different and require different chemical secretions. Therefore, to insure the most efficient digestion and best food combination possible, these three foods should not be consumed simultaneously within the same meal. They optimally are separated within different meals.

If a protein is eaten with a carbohydrate, (poor combination) such as meat and a piece of gluten-free bread or a potato in the same meal, the different digestive fluids required to break down these foods require more energy and will normally nullify each other's effectiveness. When this is done, the protein will putrefy and the carbohydrate will ferment, which will result in gas, bloat and flatulence in the body. This will increase the cellular gases within the body. Although there are those that seem to tolerate this combination they are still utilizing more energy for digestion and assimilation. This adds to your aging process.

If a protein is eaten with a sugar, such as nuts with raisins, the protein will putrefy and the sugar will ferment. This again will result in gas, bloat and flatulence in the body. This poor combination will utilize more energy for digestion and assimilation. The same is true if a carbohydrate is eaten with a sugar, such as a cooked grain with an apple or a banana.

Healthy cells and genetic structure is weakened by poor food combinations because when fermentation and putrefaction occurs Otto Warburg's research has indicated this is a form of inflammation.

Improper food combining is one of the main variables that leads to excess weight gain. The energy necessary to break down and eliminate these excesses constantly stresses the digestive system. This places an increased energy burden on the body. It leads to dysfunctions in digestion and elimination and decreased activity levels.

Proteins (concentrated foods) should be eaten together with steamed vegetables and/or with salads (high water content foods) for optimum digestion.

Carbohydrates (concentrated foods) should be eaten together with steamed vegetables and/or with salads (high water content foods) for optimum digestion.

Spinach is an excellent food and is always eaten uncooked because it contains oxalic acid which assists in the peristaltic (wavelike) actions of the intestines. Spinach is best consumed as a juice or in a salad.

Raw Tomatoes (uncooked) are an acid fruit, but when they are eaten and enter the digestive system they are highly alkaline and help neutralize acid build-up in the body. But when tomatoes are cooked, they are extremely acid-forming; so if you eat them as spaghetti sauce, (not recommended) be certain to consume a large green salad first to offset the acidity. Keep in mind, tomatoes are a member of the nightshade family and in some individuals can cause problems with joint inflammation and pain.

Liquids are consumed half an hour before a meal or 1 hour after a meal and not during or directly after a meal because this dilutes the chemical digestive secretions which causes inflammation and requires more energy output. There are some exceptions but this is based on certain individual differences.

Sprouts are a whole food source that contains enzymes, proteins, vitamins and minerals and a good source of fiber. They can be eaten raw, alone, with salads, steamed, blended, in sandwiches, soups and in a low heat stir fry.

Hormone /Antibiotic-Free Meat which is free range and grass fed is best. Consider meat a luxury and an appetizer, it is not a necessity for every meal.

Restaurant Meals When eating out, choose fresher food menu items and feel confident about telling the waiter what you want!

Food Shopping: know your menu, make a list, and read the labels. Go to the farmer's market, start a co-op, use the internet, find a good organic produce store & work with each other.

Eat: Fruits, Vegetables, Nuts, Seeds, Sprouts, Whole Grains, and small portions of Meat—all organic, if possible.

Water: Well (tested), Ionized Water, Spring/Filtered, Distilled, Reverse Osmosis. Remember, no drinking with your meals; ½ hour before or 1 hour later is fine.

Eat organic foods that are grown without the use of pesticides and chemicals.

Food Preparations: (from uncooked to most cooked): Raw, Blended, Steamed, Boiled, Baked, Broiled, Sautéed.

Fresh-Made Juices are tremendously IMPORTANT for your health. Juicers include: Norwalk which is best and most expensive, Omega is slow speed juicer and fairly price go to the website and Breville is fast speed juicer. Slower speed juices will last 2-3 days longer than fast speed juices which need to be drank within the hour of the juicing it.

Avoid Processed Foods, for the rest of your life because it removes companion nutrients and adds preservatives and chemicals for color, taste and shelf life.

Pasteurized and Homogenized Dairy are problematic products that require more energy, are less efficient and a burden to the body, cause inflammation and are associated with many health problems.

Blended salads are an excellent meal exchange for a regular salad. This is similar to a smoothie made with vegetables. Blended salads are good for people who have problems with digestion and find it hard to assimilate a regular salad.

By adhering to the rules of properly ordered food combining, the digestive system works less, thereby conserving energy that can be utilized elsewhere in the body. This conserved energy can be used by the body for the cleansing/detoxing of accumulated waste on a cellular level which will increase your performance over time.

Top 10 causes of Death: Heart, Cancer, Stroke, Lung, Accidents, Diabetes, Pneumonia/Influenza, Alzheimer's, and Kidney and Blood Diseases. 85% of all diseases are related to what we eat, breathe, and drink.

Good sleep patterns are necessary. Eating dinner before darkness or 3 hours before bed is optimal to help you sleep well. Also, closing your eyes during the day and being still/not moving (short napping) will revitalize your energy level.

Optimal Parameters: Eating smaller, dense, and high water- content foods @ 60-80% — Fruits, Veggies, Seeds, Nuts, and Sprouts (fresh and uncooked) in the form of Juices and Salads — combined with a 40-20% balance of Grains and/or minimum Meats. Prepare and consume, raw portion first then cooked portions last in this order so that the body digests and assimilates in the most energy efficient way.

Fad Diets: weight-loss schemes and standardized height weight charts based on the average western diet have led to an unhealthy population.

The critical points to remember are:

What You Leave Out

Eating & Drinking: Real, Fresh Foods

Commit to Parameters & Fine Tune for a Lifetime

By following these procedures, you will allow your body to automatically go to your optimum body weight… and remain there!

Choose Food as near as possible to its originally designed state, as it was create as a Whole Food.

Lifestyle changes take place across your whole lifetime, so understanding that process and enjoy Your Healthy Journey.

Remember:

The percentage of degenerative diseases decreases the closer you get to a lifestyle change

that includes an 80% plant-based (fruits, veggies, nuts, seeds, sprouts) and 20% protein-based (grains, legumes, & minimal animal meats, if desired).

---

6. Eating Guidelines
ORGANICALLY GROWN PRODUCE & REAL FRESH FOODS

CATEGORY	PUT IN	LEAVE OUT
Beverages (*no fluids with meals*)	Non-caffeine herbal tea (*chamomile, mint, etc.*) Fresh vegetable juices daily! Ionized, filtered or spring water	**NO:** Alcohol, cocoa, coffee, tea, fizzy drinks, canned & pasteurized juices, artificial sweetened fruit drinks, all energy drinks/ sodas
Nuts & Rice Milks (*when permitted*)	Almond, brazil nut, walnut, pistachio milks, rice milk	**NO DAIRY:** processed & imitation cheeses, butter, ice cream & toppings, pasteurized milk & milk products, colored cheeses, & margarines
Eggs (*when permitted*)	3 weekly, poached or boiled (*free range & organic*)	**NO:** Fried, hard-boiled, or pickled
Fish (*mercury free*)	Fish with fins & scales Wild salmon	**NO:** Non-white fleshed, breaded, fried fish, shellfish or fish canned in oil
Fruit (*when permitted*)	Fresh ripe fruit in season	**NO:** Canned or sweetened fruits
Grains (*when permitted*)	Brown rice, millet, buckwheat, cornmeal, amaranth, quinoa, brown rice pasta (Tinkyada), gluten-free, whole grain bread	**NO:** White flour products, hull-less grains, white pasta, white rice, cold or prepared cereals, rye, wheat, oats, barley breads, white flour crackers with hydrogenated oils.
Meat (*when permitted*)	Cow, buffalo, lamb, goat (*hormone & antibiotic free, grass-fed, organic*)	**NO:** Meat products, cold cuts, pork, hot dogs, luncheon meat, smoked, pickled & processed meats, corned beef, duck, gravies & spare ribs
Fowl	Chicken and turkey (*organic, no hormones, no antibiotics, free range*)	**NO:** Chicken or turkey cold cuts
Nuts & Seeds (*substituted for fish, chicken, or meat*)	**nuts:** Almonds, pecans, brazil nuts, macadamia, walnuts **seeds:** flax, sunflower, pumpkin, sesame. (*All nuts and seeds should be raw & unsalted.*)	**NO:** Roasted & salted nuts especially peanuts and peanut butter made with roasted peanuts

CATEGORY	PUT IN	LEAVE OUT
Seasonings *(When permitted)*	Herbs, garlic, basil, onions, chives, cumin, turmeric, marjoram, parsley, Himalayan or Celtic sea salt, raw apple cider vinegar, tamari, seaweed, dulse,	**NO:** Black or white pepper, salt, cayenne, all other vinegars, hot spices, hot red peppers
Soups	Vegetables with non-gluten grains /Brown rice, whole rice pasta, bean, lentil, pea	NO: Canned soup, fat stock, cream-thickened, packaged or dry soup
Sprouts *(Source of enzymes, vitamins, minerals, and proteins)*	Alfalfa, lentils, mung, vegetable, grains, seeds *(all complete proteins; must be fresh)*	**No:** Spoiled or moldy sprouts
Sweets	Raw honey, unsulfured blackstrap molasses, carob, pure maple syrup, stevia & agave *(small amounts only)*	**No:** Refined sugars, white or brown, turbinado, chocolate syrup, candy, sugar substitutes
Vegetables *(fresh & organic are best, eat plenty)*	Green, leafy veggies, potatoes, squash, yams, etc *(mostly uncooked, steamed, & baked)*	**No:** Canned, fried, or boiled veggies
Beans *(best sprouted)*	Fresh lentils, kidney, black, lima, and white beans, split peas, chickpeas, etc *(cooked in moderation)*	**No:** Beans cooked with animal fat
Oils **(essential fats)**	Cold-pressed, 1st pressed, olive, hemp, walnut, flaxseed, sunflower, nut & seed oils	**No:** Saturated fats, hydrogenated oils, margarine, refined processed oils, shortenings, hardened oils
Nut Butters	Nuts: almonds, pecans, brazil nuts, macadamia, walnuts seeds**:** tahini pumpkin, coconut butter (all raw butters)	**NO:** Roasted & salted nuts

It's What You Put In   AND   What You Leave Out

7. Details of What To Put In

Fruits (vitamin rich)

Oranges (all varieties), Grapefruits, Lemons, Limes, Coconuts, Grapes, Raisins, Figs, Apricots

Apples (all varieties), Pears, Peaches, Cherries, all Berries, Plums, Bananas, Kiwis, Medjool Dates

Watermelons, Melons, Cantaloupe, Cranshaw, Honeydew, Papayas, Mangoes, Pineapples

Vegetables (mineral rich)

Leafy Greens/Lettuces:

Spinach, Romaine, Chicory, Kale, Boston Bibb, Endive, Collards, Escarole, Arugula, Red Tip, Green Curley, Mesclun, Fennel, Watercress, Chard

Light Starch Salad Ingredients:

Cucumber, Celery, Red or Green Pepper, Tomato (all varieties), Zucchini, Broccoli, Cauliflower, String Beans, Asparagus, Yellow Squash, Cabbage, Okra, Avocado **Sea Vegetables:** Dulse, Kelp, Nori, Arame

Root Vegetables:

Carrots, Beets, Parsnips, Turnips

Semi-Concentrated Carbohydrate Starches:

Jerusalem Artichokes, Acorn and Butternut Squash, Corn, White and Sweet Potatoes, Yams

Grains/Concentrated Carbohydrates:

Brown Rice, Millet, Buckwheat, Cornmeal, Amaranth, Quinoa, Gluten-free Bread, Brown Rice Pasta (Tinkyada), Polenta, Kamut

Beans/ Concentrated Protein & Carbohydrate:

Fresh Lentils, Kidney and Black or White Beans, Split Peas, Lima, Chick Peas, Navy, Pinto, Etc.

Seeds & Nuts/ Protein & Fats:

Almonds, Pecans, Brazil, Macadamia Nuts, Walnuts, Sunflower, Pumpkin, Sesame, Flax Seeds

Nut Butters:

Almond Butter, Macadamia Nut Butter, Tahini

8. Recipes
Delicious Juices & Delightful Salads

STEP 1

Freshly Made Juices:

Choose one of these recipes: (Each recipe makes 8 oz; double it makes 16 oz)
♣ 2.5 oz each/ Carrot, Celery, & Apple (Yellow Delicious)
♣ 5.5 oz Carrot, 2.5 oz Celery
♣ 5.5 oz Carrot, 2.5 oz Spinach
♣ 2.5 oz each/ Carrot, Cucumber, Small Beet
♣ 2 oz each/ Carrot, Parsley, Celery, Spinach
♣ 2 oz of Romaine Lettuce & Celery, 4 oz Apple
♣ 1 Yellow Delicious Apple, ½ Lemon (peeled), plus variety of Greens: Kale, Celery, Spinach, Romaine, Peppers

STEP 2

Large Green Tossed Salad

Any combination of Greens:	Additions:	Dressings:
Romaine, chicory, kale, Boston Bibb, endive, arugula, Red Tip, collards, green curly	Tomato, sprouts, celery, peppers, cucumber, zucchini Onions and garlic *(in moderation)*	Hemp, flax oils, Raw nut oils, Extra virgin olive oil Raw Apple cider Lemon Himalayan/Celtic Salt (in moderation)

9. Food Combining

It is essential to follow the principles of correct food combinations, eaten at the proper times, in the correct order to enjoy effortless digestion and assimilation that will lead you to optimum health, energy, and well-being. The body's biochemistry works in the most efficient manner when the proper food combinations, times and order are applied, and this is the main reason I advocate this approach—I want your body to be working for you in the healthiest way possible, which will give you the most beneficial potential lifestyle change.

Incompatible food combinations will only require more energy output and eventually express a genetic weakness. You can eat a variety of plant-based foods but they will be eaten in separate meals. Mixing incompatible foods and eating them together at the same meal will take away from the health of your body.

- **Fruit should eaten alone as a separate plateful of food and not mixed with any protein or starch/carbohydrate.**

- **Fruits can be mixed with leafy green vegetables, celery, cucumber as a Blended Meal Only.**

- Acid fruits and sub-acid fruits can be eaten together as a serving and should be finished first, and then sweet fruits may be followed as an additional portion.

- All melons should be eaten alone as a separate meal for optimal usage and to prevent flatulence.

- Protein and starches/carbohydrates should not be eaten in the same meal.

- Proteins may be eaten with leafy green vegetables and light starch vegetables in the same course as a meal.

- Starches/carbohydrates may be eaten with leafy green vegetables and light starch vegetables in the same course as a meal.

(See Food Combining Chart on the next page)

LEAFY GREEN VEGETABLES AND LIGHT STARCH VEGETABLES
(Carrots, beets, artichokes, peas, string beans, broccoli, cauliflower)

↕**YES** **YES**↕

PROTEIN/VEGETABLES

Raw Nuts
Raw Seeds
Nut-Butters (Raw)
Seed-Butters (Raw)
Soybeans
Fish
Fowl
Meat

◄ PROTEIN/STARCH ►

NO

STARCH/VEGETABLES

Potatoes, Sweet, Yams
Grains
  Brown Rice, Barley, Kasha, Millet,
  Cracked Wheat, Whole Wheat,
  Quinoa, Amaranth, Kamut
Pasta
  Gluten Free, Brown Rice, Spelt,
  Quinoa, Corn Gluten, Whole Wheat
Dried Beans and Peas
Winter Squash
Pumpkin
Chestnuts

◄ NO SWEET ► **NO** ◄ NO ACID ►

ACID FRUIT

Blackberries
Grapefruit
Kumquat
Lemon
Lime
Orange
Pineapple
Plums (sour)
Pomegranates
Raspberries
Sour Apples
Strawberries
Tangerines
Tangelos

◄**YES**► Acid/sub-acid

SUB-ACID FRUIT

Apple
Apricot
Blueberries
Cherimoya
Cherries
Fresh Fig
Grapes
Huckleberries
Kiwi
Mango
Nectarine
Peach
Pear
Plums (sweet)

◄**YES**► Sub-acid/sweet

SWEET FRUIT

Bananas
Dates
Dried Fruit
Grapes (Thomson)
Persimmons
Raisins

**Sweet Fruit should
be eaten AFTER
Sub-acid fruit

MELONS:
Canteloupe, Casaba,
Honey Dew, Water
Melon, Crenshaw,
Persian, etc.
**MUST BE EATEN
ALONE!**

** Melons MUST be eaten ALONE
** Sweet Fruit should be eaten AFTER
  Sub-Acid Fruit

Your Healthy Journey Fred's Food Pyramid

Raw Desserts: 1-2X/Week/
Freshly Prepared Whole Foods

Supplements:
Systemic Enzymes, Digestive Enzymes
Probiotics, Vitamin D, Vitamin B12

Teas / Organic
Herbal, No Caffeine

Spices (In Moderation)
(No Pepper or Hot Spices)
Himalayan or Celtic Salt, Garlic,
Cumin, Turmeric, Etc.

Animal Protein/ Organic
(If desired but Not-Essential or Needed)
(Omit on a Vegan Lifestyle)
Grass-fed Beef or Free-range Chicken
Eggs in moderation in place of animal protein
Can be used in place of one Fish Meal

Essential Fats (Cold Pressed)
Extra Virgin Olive Oil, Hemp,
Flax, Coconut, Walnut, Avocado

Fish/2-3X/Week/
(Mercury free) (If desired but Not-Essential)
(Omit on a Vegan Lifestyle)
Wild Salmon, Wild Black Cod, Sardines

Beans & Legumes / Whole Unprocessed Grains (Non-Gluten)

Raw Seeds: Chia, Hemp, / Raw Nuts: Walnuts, Pine & Brazil Nuts
Sesame, Sunflower & Pumpkin / Macadamia, Almonds, Pistachio. Etc.

| Fresh Juices | / | Green Smoothies |
| & Blended Salads | / | & Super Green Powders |

Vegetables (Organic if possible)	/	Fruit
Large Variety, Mostly Raw Vegetables	/	(Organic if possible)
with some steamed Vegetables	/	Large Variety of Fruits
Including some Raw Sprouts	/	including Avocados

Vegan Whole Food Lifestyle works well if desired, done correctly
100% Raw Plant Food Lifestyle works if done correctly

10. Intermediate Level Lifestyle/Menu

The Intermediate Level eating lifestyle is the one that is suitable for most people who are starting to make a lifestyle change. When, what, and how you eat, directly determines your body's ability to function in the most efficient manner which will give you the best energy output and genetic expression.

PLEASE REMEMBER:

✓ Lunch/Dinner- always follow the sequence of choices—1 before 2, 2 before 3!

✓ Most optimally, each serving of food associated with each choice should be eaten in its entirety before you move on to the next choice.

✓ (For example, if you choose 4 servings for your noon meal vegetable juice, 2. Salad, 3. Steamed vegetables, then choose one choice as a cooked portion, ex. 4. Rice and beans—follow the dishes in sequence and eat each choice in its entirety. This means: drink your juice first in its entirety, eat and finish your salad to completion, then eat your steamed vegetables till they are done, and then eat the rice & beans.)

✓ Pick one for your morning meal means pick one only.

✓ Always stick to eating only three meals a day and no eating solid foods/snacks between meals.

✓ Follow proper combinations and sequence/order.

✓ Optimal parameters are eating smaller, dense, water-plump foods. This includes 60-80%, fruits, vegetables, seeds, nuts, and sprouts (fresh and uncooked) in the form of juices and salads combined with a 40-20% balance of grain/meat cooked portioned meals.

Again, following the order and sequence lets the body digest and assimilate in the most energy efficient way which creates and sustains better function, systemically.

The percentage of degenerative diseases decreases and your performance increases the closer you get to a lifestyle that includes 80% fruit, vegetable, nuts, seeds and sprouts and 20% protein, grains and legumes, with all foods as near as possible to their original state, as designed by nature— REAL, FRESH FOOD.

Your Healthy Journey is a lifestyle change for the rest of your life. So don't be confused by fad weight-loss schemes and standardized height-weight charts based on the average western diets which have led to wide-spread ill health.

Please remember, this is a **lifestyle change**, not a diet that you just go on and off as you please. Every time you make a diet or a lifestyle change in your life you make a change in your body's chemistry and physiology. These yo-yo effects will affect you physically over time, so setting up realistic parameters is the key to maintaining the kind of consistency that will allow you to stay with this lifetime process and enjoy the best possible health.

The 3 critical points to remember are:

1. BE DILIGENT ABOUT **WHAT YOU LEAVE OUT**

2. EAT & DRINK **REAL, FRESH FOODS**

3. **COMMIT TO YOUR INDIVIDUAL PARAMETERS**, ADJUST/FINE TUNE OVER YOUR LIFETIME, THEN RECOMMIT TO YOUR NEW PARAMETERS

Follow these precepts and your body will automatically go to its optimum weight/functionality for your desired determined performance and goals. Lifestyle changes take place across your whole lifetime, so be understanding and compassionate with yourself and enjoy Your Healthy Journey.

PLEASE NOTE: Consult your physician before you begin. I strongly suggest that you seek guidance and supervision so that you can benefit from the experience of a professional so you proceed in a safe manner.

INTERMEDIATE LEVEL LIFESTYLE/MENU - 3 MEALS/DAY

Morning Meal		Morning Meal
PICK ONE NUMBER ONLY FROM 1 TO 5	1.	**Fresh Fruit** (up to 1 pound/2-3 pieces). Use a variety of fruits from meal to meal. Option: Can be followed with 2 oz. of **raw nuts** (small handful) 30 minutes after fruit.
	2.	**Fresh Vegetable Juice** (8-12 oz.). Can be followed by 4 oz. of **raw nuts** *(soak nuts)*
PICK ONE NUMBER ONLY FROM 1 TO 5	3.	**Whole Grains** (4 oz. dry weight) Steamed or cooked in water. brown rice, millet, quinoa buckwheat, corn meal.(gluten free) Option: (when permitted) nut/rice milks can be added
	4.	**Blended Almond/Walnut/Brazil Drink** 16 oz. water with 1 large handful blanched nuts *(soak nuts)* 1 Medjool date or agave to taste
	5.	**Blended Green Smoothie**—blend coconut or regular water with fruit and greens, lettuce and celery or **Coconut kefir** or **nut kefir**
Noon Meal		Noon Meal
EAT 1, 2, <u>and</u> 3 *in that order*	1.	**Fresh vegetable Juice** (8-12 oz.)
	2.	**Large Green Salad** consisting of Romaine lettuce, cucumber, celery, peppers plus 2 additional veggies (Sprouts- great addition)
	3.	**Steamed vegetables**. Pick a minimum of two & eat as much as desired (but no overeating!)
		Plus pick one of the following:
PICK ONE NUMBER ONLY FROM 4 to 9	4.	**Raw Nuts** (4 oz.): almonds, brazil, pecans, pumpkin/ sunflower seeds, pistachio, walnuts or macadamia. *(soak nuts)*
	5.	**Grains:** Brown rice, Basmati brown rice, millet, buckwheat, quinoa, cornmeal or Tinkyada Pasta. (Option: mix with veggies)
	6.	**Potatoes:** White, sweet or yams (3/4 lb.)
	7.	**Squash:** Acorn, Butternut, Spaghetti (3/4 lb).
	8.	**Beans:** Lentils, Lima Beans, Mung Beans, Chick Peas. *(Sprouted beans can be added)*
	9.	**Wheat and Gluten-free bread**, 7 Grain Sprouted bread (when allowed) with avocado, lettuce & tomato or vegetables

INTERMEDIATE LEVEL LIFESTYLE/MENU - 3 MEALS/DAY

Evening Meal		Evening Meal *eaten 3 hours before bed or dark*
EAT 1, 2, & 3 *in that order*	1.	**Fresh vegetable Juice** (8-12 oz.)
	2.	**Large Green Salad** consisting of romaine lettuce, cucumber, celery, peppers plus two additional vegetables OR **Blended Green Salad** (16 oz) consisting of Romaine lettuce, cucumber, celery, peppers, tomato, **plus**… **fruit** (small quantity only) **or avocado**
	3.	**Steamed vegetables.** Pick a minimum of two & eat as much as desired (but no overeating!)
		Plus pick one of the following:
PICK ONE NUMBER ONLY FROM 4 to 11	4.	**Raw Nuts** (4 oz.): almonds, brazil, pecans, pumpkin/sunflower seeds, pistachio, walnuts or macadamia. *(soak nuts)* OR flax/raw crackers
	5.	**Tinkyada Pasta** (non-meat sauce) 3X/week maximum (option: mix with veggies)
	6.	**Potatoes:** white, sweet or yams (3/4 lb.).
	7.	**Squash:** Acorn, Butternut, Spaghetti (3/4 lb).
	8.	**Brown rice and Beans** (2/3 rice & 1/3 beans) "Do not overeat"
	9.	**Fish** (4-6 oz.) Steamed, broiled or baked. (No shell fish)
	10.	**Chicken** (4-6 oz.) Steamed, broiled or baked
	11.	**Turkey/Cow** (4-6 oz.) **all animal proteins eaten only 3x/week max. Choosing meat one day for one meal only every other day! Do not eat starch/carbohydrate & animal protein at the same meal. Animal protein can be eaten as a lunch/dinner meal option.**

ADVANCED LEVEL RAW LIFESTYLE/MENU—2/3 MEALS/DAY

Morning Meal		Morning Meal
PICK ONE NUMBER ONLY FROM 1 to 6	1.	**Fresh Fruit** (up to 1 pound/2-3 pieces). Use a variety of fruits from meal to meal. Can be followed with 2 oz. of **raw nuts** (small handful) ½ hour after fruit.
	2.	**Fresh vegetable Juice** (8-12 oz.). Can be followed by 4 oz. of **raw nuts** (soak nuts)
	3.	**Fermented vegetable** or Kim Chi—add avocado & hemp oil
	4.	**Blended almond Drink** 16 oz. water with 1 large handful blanched nuts *(soak nuts)* 1 Medjool date or agave to taste.
	5.	Blended **green smoothie**—blend coconut or regular water with fruit and greens, lettuce & celery
	6.	**coconut kefir** or nut milk kefir
Noon Meal		**Noon Meal**
PICK ONE NUMBER 1 TO 6	1.	a) **Fresh vegetable/greens juice** (8-12 oz.) b) **Large green salad** consisting of Romaine lettuce, cucumber, celery, peppers **plus: sprouts or raw soaked nuts** (2-3 oz.) **or avocado.**
	2.	**Blended green salad** (16 oz) consisting of Romaine lettuce, cucumber, celery, peppers, tomato, **plus -Fruit** (small q**uantity) or avocado can be followed by Flax or raw crackers**
	3.	**raw soup** with **flax/raw crackers**
	4.	**coconut Kefir** over **fresh fruit**
	5.	**Fermented vegetable** or Kim Chi—add **hemp oil** & **avocad**o or **flax/raw crackers**
	6.	One item from the **breakfast menu**
Evening Meal		**Evening Meal** *eaten 3 hours before bed or dark*
PICK ONE NUMBER ONLY FROM 1 to 3	1.	Pick one **morning meal**
	2.	Pick one **noon meal**
	3.	Pick one **raw dessert** (2 X/week max.)
		try not to overeat—this can be a problem with a raw lifestyle

"IF YOU GET OUT OF THE WAY THE BODY WILL DO THE HEAVY LIFTING"

PART III
The Process

Healing & Regeneration

W hen you improve your eating, drinking, and general lifestyle, you will receive many signs confirming that you're on the right path: improvement of degenerative health conditions, rejuvenated immune system, improved concentration, sharpened thinking, younger skin and appearance, extended lifespan, reduced stress and sleep, improved athletic performance and a slowing of the aging process. You will see, feel, think, and perform better than ever before.

Following Your Healthy Journey allows you the potential to regain your health. This outcome is achieved by establishing good habits in the following areas: food combinations, sequencing of foods (most easily digested foods followed by a moderate amount of concentrated foods), quality and quantity of food consumed in each meal and the timing and frequency of eating a meal (when you're hungry rather than by the clock and no eating less than three-four hours before bed or too early in the morning).

The dedication you apply will reveal remarkable results for the body and the mind. The amazing intelligence that is present in every cell of the body expresses the multiple variables of cellular chemistry and physiology that works together to manifest these remedial healing capabilities. As you feed your body properly (**what you put in**) by following the principles of **what you leave out**, you give the cells an opportunity to detoxify, cleanse and eliminate from the tissues, systemically. This opens up cell unburdening and utilization of nutrients to rebuild and develop healthier tissue.

If we create optimum conditions for the body, it will always seek health on every level, from its macro functions all the way down to the individual cell. We see this phenomenon in the self-healing nature of the body when it is confronted with colds, fevers, cuts, and swellings—in other words, illness and injury of any kind. What inhibits this natural healing process is depriving the body of the optimum conditions by returning to your previous ways of just existing. This is why it cannot be overemphasized that you need to make a commitment to a lifestyle change and then live within your parameters; it is the only way your body can regain its health and maintain it throughout your lifetime.

EXPERIENCING THE ADJUSTMENTS

When you start Your Healthy Journey the body must go through phases of chemical adjustment that arise from the elimination of waste products within the cells (toxic endogenous cellular materials). For example, when the use of any stimulant such as coffee, tea, or chocolate is suddenly stopped, headaches are common while the caffeine and associated theobromine endotoxins are removed from the cells and discarded by the body into the bloodstream during its many circulatory cycles. The toxins then exit the body via the intestines, kidneys, lungs and the skin. During this process, detoxification symptoms (aches and pains) may occur and there may also be a feeling of tiredness when the body is deprived of stimulants. This lifestyle change— elimination of stimulating drinks—in turn can produce a slower heart rate that causes a reduction of activity level which you may perceive as an energy letdown. During these periods of chemical adjustment, when the body goes through a process of adaptation, the motto is: Rest is Best. Usually within three days the detox symptoms will fade and you will feel stronger as a result of the physical recuperation that follows the adaptation.

Another example is leaving out processed products and replacing them with *Real, Fresh Foods*. Processed foods which are subjected to chemical treatment, additives, spices, preservatives, commercial salt and other harmful alterations cause unhealthy levels of stimulation to the body. This is your opportunity for cleansing. If you also combine leaving out or consuming only a moderate amount of concentrated protein from animals—meat, chicken, or fish —this will decrease the stimulation and create a change in Chemistry again. Consequently, a reduction in your consumption of animal protein in exchange for less concentrated plant-based protein (beans, nuts, seeds & whole grains) produces a slower heart rate which registers as relaxation and tiredness. This relaxation phase may last from three to ten days or slightly longer. It is then followed by an increase in strength and a feeling of greater well-being. This transitional bodily change is an expression of the body's skill at cleaning you up on a cellular level.

LIFETIME PROCESS OF REGENERATION

Once you have made this commitment to Your Healthy Journey, you will experience these relaxation phases over your lifetime. You might sometimes interpret this as a weakness but don't be tempted to go back to your former habits because you body needs time to adapt to these periods of adjustments. Realize this is a long lifetime view and you will understand why it is vital to allow the body to follow through with these chemical and physiological corrections every time that your body adapts. Let the body adapt and the rewards will follow.

Just keep in mind that when you have any temporary feeling of weakness, catabolism, it's very important to increase your vegetable/green juices, get additional rest and sleep, decrease activities, stop wasting energy by using muscular movement or taking stimulants and try skipping some solid food meals.

You could lose faith at this point but when you stay with it you are now opening your healing pathways. Be patient.

If you listen carefully to your body, it will tell you what's going on. When your body speaks, listen.

Remember, the Recuperation, Stabilization and Regeneration phases is the ongoing adventure of Your Healthy Journey to optimal health. It is an expression of the miraculous fact that the body was created to always intelligently seek health, if it is given the opportunity. The key is to have the **patience** and **faith** to stay within your parameters and listen to your body.

Success in recovering and improving your health hinges upon this understanding. Realize that the body must go through this physical, tangible experience by withdrawing its energies from external activities involving muscle movements in order to utilize its main energies in the more important internal work is an important awareness.

So whenever phase you are in, be wise, be aware, take it easy, and relax. We suggest that you just **coast,** until you're out of the woods.

After a while you'll notice your strength will increase and will ultimately far exceed anything you have experienced before. You will start to realize a build-up of energy increasing, your weight will stabilize, even though you are consuming fewer calories.

So maintaining Your Healthy Journey **(consistently)** means leaving out the processed foods, improving the quality of the foods you consume, knowing the right quantity, following the proper food combinations and sequencing, then you will facilitate the regeneration of cells which will improve everything systemically.

As this lifetime regeneration of cells takes place, your body will deal with the build-up in the cells of endogenous materials created throughout a lifetime of poor eating and living habits through detoxification. But there are also the continual exogenous materials that need handling. The origin of exogenous materials is the foods and products we consume and the environment we live in. These two processes can be going on and they can conflict with each other. So be aware of the detoxification from elimination and the intoxication from over consumption of concentrated foods and food in general.

Also, we are all different within our own genetic and structural makeup, these weaknesses can leave our cells open to certain vulnerabilities. This, combined with the effect of previous habits that led us to take in exogenous toxins and store them endogenously, can affect cells in the organs, circulatory, digestive, and musculoskeletal systems in multiple ways. It can decrease or increase functionality, which results in exhaustion, overproduction, and the need for stimulation. The result is excess, sludge, masses, and deposits that the body wants to eliminate so it can get healthy and enjoy the optimal state of well-being.

Again, the point to understand is that the body focuses its energy internally, and symptoms of this are muscle weakness/tiredness and mental fatigue. This process of elimination starts in the cells and follows various pathways via the liver, intestines, kidneys, lungs and the skin. The body's housecleaning process can include the skin breaking out, headaches, intolerance to cold, increased temperature, short intervals of loose or sluggish bowel movements, foul-smelling stool, feelings of tiredness or weakness, muscular and joint discomfort/achiness, disinclination to exercise, nervousness, irritability, mental negativity, frequent urination, gas, nausea, bloated stomach, dripping nose, recurrence of past discomforts, weight loss, foul breath, aggravated throat, nasal congestion, sudden cough, mucus discharge, sensations of cravings and addictions, mood changes, loss of appetite, and body odor.

These bodily housecleaning actions may be unpleasant but these periods are constructive over the long term and are part of the healing process the body performs.

It should be mentioned that the progress of these bodily housecleaning processes/experiences, which lead to cellular regeneration, can decrease and even cease altogether, if you consume or expose yourself to stimulating exogenous materials. These exogenous materials can include anything that causes a stimulation to your body. These would include alcohol, caffeine, concentrated or refined foods or anything from the "what you leave out" list, **massive** doses of vitamins, over-consuming food or not following food combinations and sequencing, correctly.

These short-lived periods, conditions and manifestations are showing you how your body is leading you to health. So staying within the parameters of eating properly in quality, quantity, combinations, sequence, and **what you're leaving out** helps you understand that these bodily processes are temporary in nature; through each experience you go through, you will gain greater **faith**, **strength**, **poise** and **promise**.

The body follows an ordered pathway to health which first involves **spiritual faith** (the belief in what you're doing), followed by **bodily strength** (the transitory regeneration period that leads you to physical vigor), and then **emotional mental confidence** (state of well-being).

Here is where my sixty years of personal and clinical experience is of great value to you, because I have learned how to show people to live that life as an individual from my own living example (I walk the talk). Be happy and learn as you go; maturity will follow because you're on the easy installment elimination plan. **You'll be paying back a little bit at a time.**

LEARNING FROM YOUR PAST EXPERIENCES

What can I learn from the past, now that I'm eating better than I ever did before? As you eat better, the rate of recurrence and degrees of Regeneration are determined by your past experiences (retracing your past). In your meals, you may be observing the principles of quality, quantity, food combining, and sequence, within your parameters and yet uncomfortable bodily processes will still occur. Generally, those who have made previous lifestyle changes throughout their lives by eating real fresh foods and still having stimulating lifestyles in moderation, will experience different rates of recurrence and degrees of Regeneration than those who have only just started making lifestyles changes (this helps you measure your parameters). A lifestyle routine such as overeating will range from no reaction to mild reactions to various stimulations of bodily processes. During this lifestyle change you are always learning and becoming aware of what your body is trying to say to you. By paying attention, this becomes less of a routine and more of Your Healthy Journey.

The bodily processes will vary according to the waste products stored within the cells (endogenous materials) that are discarded, the condition of the organs involved in the elimination, and the amount of energy you have available. The more you rest/sleep and decrease your activities when these bodily processes are present, the milder they are and the more quickly they are carried out. Those that have more stimulating bodily processes and follow through to their successful termination will realize with certainty that their body is becoming younger and healthier. The great majorities of people find their reactions tolerable and are encouraged to bear and endure with them. The many health improvements that will occur will become more evident each day. This will build your self-reliance.

The numerous stories asserting that the body will feel increasingly better once you improve your eating habits—in other words, form a consistently ascending scale of quality and health until perfection is reached—is a **myth**. The **reality** is that the body is cyclical in nature and that health returns in a series of gradually diminishing cycles.

Life is an ongoing story, so once upon a time, you started Your Healthy Journey and for a while you felt much better. After some point in time, bodily processes started to occur—you may have experienced nausea for a day and had loose bowel movements with a foul-smelling stool. After a day, you felt greatly improved and all went well for a while. Then, unexpectedly you experienced intolerance to cold and lost your appetite. After about two or three days (assuming you didn't take massive doses of vitamins, stimulants, overeat, or fail to follow food combinations, got plenty of rest/ sleep with a decrease in muscle movement & social activities) you suddenly recovered and felt better than you did for years.

Now, let's say this well-being continued for two months and then you noticed that your skin was breaking out and you didn't use any outside stimulus. Then the skin flare up intensified, stayed that way for ten days, and then subsided. Immediately after this, your energy increased more than ever before. Then over some extended period of time, you experience nausea, loose bowel movements, foul smelling stool, and intolerance to cold and loss of appetite and then vibrant health returned—Wow, what a ride but nevertheless you made it by letting your body go through these changes that brought you, where you needed to go!

Congratulations, you have just experienced Regeneration through Elimination. This is how recovery occurs—cyclical in nature with gradually diminishing cycles as the body seeks health for your physical benefit and well-being. You cycle into good health, then you experience elimination and you don't feel as well for a short while. You then recover and get a regular good night's sleep. So it goes on, with each experience milder than the last, with each becoming shorter in duration and followed by longer periods of vibrant health.

You have given yourself a chance to experience what it means to be really healthy and fully alive, to feel the joy of living by the God-given remedial healing capabilities of the body to always seek health. This is what is intended for all people that want to take Your Healthy Journey.

"LIFE IS THE LONG RUN, STEP BY STEP"

PART IV

The Practice

The Foundation

MY SPIRITUAL JOURNEY

I am always asked how my journey connects me to God? Well, in order to address it correctly, I'd like to go back a little bit to my beginning, many years ago, back to the thirties and early forties. What happened then was something that shaped the rest of my life. It helped me understand what's going on in a person's mind and heart.

It just so happens I got thrown out of every school I went to. I couldn't read in the fifth grade—I was dyslexic and I was classified as being learning disabled. Also, I couldn't speak clearly; I had a pretty bad speech impediment, which I still hear, that sounds like a heavy Brooklyn accent.

So I really didn't have much hope for my life, and as a result I focused all my energies on my physical body. Realizing there was no chance for me to become any kind of an intellectual, I poured my heart and soul into sports like power weight training and boxing. Through this, I discovered I was a very committed and disciplined type of a person, and I succeeded in whatever pursuit I focused on. I was beginning to realize that my academic challenges, given the physical prowess I was developing, were perhaps not such a bad thing after all.

Then I had an experience that challenged my beliefs about what I had achieved and the importance I gave to the physical body. I ran into someone who was a blessing to me, an African-American boxing coach, and a really great guy. What that man did for me was support me spiritually by helping me see that the spiritual part of any activity is more important than the physical part. He turned everything around for me and, from that time on, it's been my spiritual life that empowers me, not my worldly life.

I've tried many approaches in my search for Truth, but the strength that I've gotten from the spiritual approach has been just awesome. It's played a larger role in my life's work than anything else I've done.

It's funny, I started life thinking I was going to be a loser, but in the end I realized God had given me a gift with which I could help others. I discovered what a blessing it was to be a blessing to other people.

Despite my poor start at school, I ended up doing very well. I've had two careers in my life and earned my master's pilot's license. I find it important to think of life as if you were a warrior because the life we live is an ongoing experience full of many different problems, diseases, and disappointments, but if you are grounded and you have a very strong faith that empowers you, with each struggle you encounter, you will become a stronger person. If you quit and succumb to the struggle, you'll be a weaker person. So my advice is to seek spiritual strength first and foremost. In my life, I have found that spiritual muscle is infinitely more powerful than physical muscle.

YOUR MIND & YOUR BELIEF SYSTEM

Enjoying and understanding Your Healthy Journey is the only way you are going to be successful. So you must be aware that your spiritual beliefs, your thoughts and feelings, the food you eat and drink, the chemicals you are exposed to in your food, water, air and environment, all have an influence on your quality of life and your genetic expression.

Often, people come to see me for help with psychological ailments like depression or anxiety, or physical illnesses like diabetes, arthritis, cancer, etc. They tell me it runs in their family and since they consider the problem to be genetically based, they are not convinced that changing their nutritional lifestyle will help or that their remedial healing capabilities of the body will not operate in their case.

Unfortunately, when somebody is already firmly convinced that they cannot be helped, most likely they aren't going to be helped. The change they're hoping for, but don't truly believe in, requires more than just improving their lifestyle, diet and weeding out all the things that interfere with a healthy physiology. It requires giving their body a chance to utilize what I believe is their God-given capability to heal themselves; but a person's negative beliefs and thoughts does interfere with this self-healing process by adversely affecting their chemistry and genetic expression.

Your mind is extremely powerful. You probably know individuals who are fearful of getting sick and always imagine they have some type of disease or illness. They read about some syndrome in the newspaper, or see it on television, and before long they have a few of the symptoms and are sure they have the disease. Another example of the power of the mind over the body is when you experience a lot of mental stress and are unable to sleep, and your immune system is suppressed. Now a lot of energy is being expended by the brain and your body thinks you're in the fight or flight response. When that happens, all the vital energy that is needed for proper bodily functioning and the healing process is diverted to this emergency response and, if this continues, your health deteriorates.

We see a similar process at work with people who are constantly worrying about the worst things that can happen—the next terrorist attack, the dangers their children face, and so on. All these types of thinking will have an effect on their genetic expression. Although, I'm not suggesting that you shouldn't have concern, what I am saying is that you can learn how to deal with all the circumstances of your life so that you feel fulfilled even under trying conditions. This means that the stress you deal with will not damage your immune system.

I know of people who have gone to doctors and been told that they have one year to live, and they accepted this pronouncement as a death sentence. Guess what happened—they died right on schedule. To me, this is a tragedy. The mind can kill you and it can keep you alive. **Why not choose life?**

So don't turn your mind into your enemy by believing that your health challenges are genetically caused, and thus there is no hope for you. Old school genetics held that the DNA controlled the outcome of illness except when something of unknown origin happened by chance. But the latest epigenetic studies show that only 5% of degenerative diseases in our society are actually genetic, whereas 95% are epigenetic. These "epigenetic" switches are outside the cell and what these studies are saying is that an amazing 95% of our diseases are controlled by what happens outside of the body —by our lifestyle ,diet, chemicals that are in our food, water, the air we breathe but mainly by the state of our **mind and spirit.**

So you have to be attentive to your belief system. If you read the newspapers or watch television, even if you don't have a conscious impression about it, it may still have a detrimental effect on your health. You may unconsciously tell yourself, "What's the sense of me trying to do anything that's positive? No matter what I do, it's just going to end up being destroyed by what's happening in the world today."

If you're looking at events in the Middle East, you'll assume there has got to be something terribly wrong because people over there are killing each other in the name of God. How could God possibly be blessing this waste of human life? All this hatred in the world, what effect is it having on our genetic expression?

Even politics in this country can affect our genetic expression. Well… I'm not a very politically oriented person but I do hope that we will have more enlightened people getting into political positions so better choices are made in government so as a country, we have a positive influence on the politics of other nations and on the peoples of the world in general. I can only hope!

GENETIC EXPRESSION

Returning to the subject of epigenetics and how it relates to lifestyle, let's now examine this in a little more detail. From information based on decades of research and my clinical practice, we know that the human cell is controlled by environmental signals. So inside the cell there are regulatory proteins that are altered by these environmental signals which then enable the cell to admit a signal response. In addition to the regulatory proteins, the DNA and RNA (the mirror image of DNA), are responding by manipulating proteins in order to control the genetic expression of the cell. What happens is that the regulatory protein exposes the nucleus of the cell so that the information coming from the outside can have an effect on your genetic expression on the inside. These epigenetic switches can go both ways; cause disease and in beneficial ways enhance your immune system and prevent disease.

When the latter occurs, the cell has the ability to replicate itself and to alter your genetic expression for the better based on the environmental signals it received. Critical among the environmental signals are your **spiritual beliefs** and the **thoughts** that you entertain, which you should strive to keep hopeful and optimistic. In contradiction, if you live in a toxic environment—in your mind, body, spirit, and world— then you're like a fish swimming in a lake filled with poisons. Your very survival is in question.

Of course, the human body is a fantastic created biological machine that has the ability to do things that are almost unbelievable. Designed to continually regenerate and heal itself, even when subjected to tremendous abuse. But the body has its limits, and in today's world most of us have reached them. We may think we're doing fine, because our life expectancy has increased dramatically over the last 150 years but it used to be that living to the age of 50 was an achievement, whereas nowadays people routinely live to be 80 or 90 years old.

However, I believe that we are really only scratching the surface. If we can clean up the outside environment and the inside environment (with a cleansing lifestyle), and if we can unite mentally and break free of our attachment of the old thought patterns that make us believe in the statistical data concerning death and disease (which, because of the influence of the mind on the body, acts as a self-fulfilling prophecy), then we can access untapped possibilities of health and longevity that few people ever dreamed of.

I would like to inspire you with the message that the discoveries I have made in my own life apply equally to yours. You can take back control; you can change what you believe and think more quickly than you may imagine. As a result you can change your life very rapidly in amazing ways. It's not something that can easily be described. You must have the experience of this wonderful enlightened consciousness for yourself, and then you will understand.

You don't have to travel to India or go to Tibet to evolve spiritually. It is a gift that we are all meant to have, right here, right now—wherever we are and whatever our circumstances. All you have to do is declare that you are a willing participant in your own healing and enlightenment, that you want a clear mind, a true sense of wellbeing, the vibrancy and vital force that the human body is meant to have, and the awareness of the divine that is your birthright.

Take this one step, and Life will take the next one thousand steps for you. My hope and intention is that this book has succeeded in inspiring you to take that first step, and to go forward on your quest. Once you have tasted a small part of the spiritual feast that is offered, you'll be convinced that this is the right path for you, and your mind, body, and spirit will be fully engaged in Your Healthy Journey. You will have an experience of awakening that will be joyful and you will want to share this not only with your loved ones but with everyone you come into contact.

You'll experience the feeling I have when I see people who are suffering physically or emotionally, and I know in my heart of hearts that they do not have to experience this—a feeling of great compassion and a desire to reach out and help them. What I wish for you is Godspeed. I pray that you receive the message in this book with an open mind and that you step forward into the incredible experience that is awaiting you.

I pray that you can now be free to change your life and inspire other people to change theirs as you set out on this amazing path that I call Your Healthy Journey, whose goal is health and wellbeing on all levels, I wish you the very best of providence, peace and happiness while you enjoy this lifetime experience!

GOD BLESS YOU

"The human condition is spiritually and vibrationally induced, electrically and chemically empowered, and biologically and genetically expressed."

Dr. Fred Bisci

Please visit us at www.anydoubtleaveitout.com

APPENDIX

Daily Meditations

LIFE IS YOUR HEALTHY JOURNEY

You will receive a body. It will be yours for an entire lifetime.

You will learn lessons. You are enrolled in a full-time informal school called Life. Each day in this school you will have the opportunity to learn lessons. You may like the lessons or think them irrelevant and stupid.

There are no mistakes, only lessons. Growth is a process of trial and error: experimentation. The 'failed' experiments are as much a part of the process as the experiment that ultimately 'works.'

A lesson is repeated until it is learned. A lesson will be presented to you in various forms until you have learned it. When you have learned it, you can then go on to the next lesson.

Learning lessons does not end. There is no part of life that does not contain its lessons. If you are alive, there are lessons to be learned.

"There" is nothing better than "being here". When your "there" has become a "here", you will simply obtain another "there" that will again look better than "here".

Others are merely mirrors of you. You cannot love or hate something about another person unless it reflects something you love or hate about yourself.

What you make of your life is up to you. You have all the tools and resources you need. What you do with them is up to you. The choice is yours.

Your answers lie inside of you. The answers to Life's questions are inside you. All you need to do is observe, listen, trust and have faith.

You will forget all this.

You can remember whenever you want.

Food For Your Thoughts

The greatest sin
Fear

The best day
Today

The biggest fool
The person who will not see that every experience is a opportunity to learn

The best town
Where you succeed

The most agreeable companion
One who would not have you any different than what you are

The great bore
One who will not come to the point

The still greater bore
One who keeps on talking after he has made his point

The greatest deceiver
One who deceives himself

The greatest invention of the devil
War

The greatest secret of production
Eliminating waste

The best work
What you like

The best play
Work

The cheapest, stupidest and easiest thing to do
Finding fault

The greatest comfort
> *The knowledge that you have done your work well*

The greatest mistake
> *Giving up*

The most expensive indulgence
> *Hate*

The greatest trouble maker
> *One who talks too much*

The greatest stumbling block
> *Egotism*

The most ridiculous asset
> *Pride*

The worst bankrupt
> *The soul that has lost its enthusiasm*

The most dangerous person
> *The liar*

The most disagreeable person
> *The complainer*

The meanest feeling of which any human being is capable
> *Feeling bad at another's success*

The cleverest man
> *One who always does what he thinks is right*

The greatest need
> *Common sense*

The greatest puzzle
> *Life*

The greatest mystery
> *Death*

The greatest teacher
> *God*

The greatest thing, bar none, in all the world
> *Love*

QUESTIONS
&
Answers

Questions and Answers

#1 Fred's Healthy Journey

You've been doing this for over fifty years, so how's Your Health Journey going?

There really isn't anything I can't do that a forty-year old person can do—run, hike, play sports, and so on. Over the years, I've completed eighteen marathons, two ultra marathons, was Olympic style weightlifter and boxer. Presently, it spite of some permanent physical damage from accidents, I'm still strong and lead an athletic life. If I have to help somebody carry a refrigerator up a flight of stairs, I can do that. I feel wonderful.

But beyond the physical aspect, there is the emotional, mental, and spiritual—the body is a big part of this unified system. I have a clear, healthy and energized body and this has benefited all the non-physical areas of my life tremendously. I must say and I pray every day to God about how well I function at the level that I do and feel this good. Being born in 1929, in good health, able-minded and going into my ninth decade, it's just fantastic!

#2 Going at your own Pace

I like the idea of my body cleaning up and getting healthy, but I want to go slowly. Is that doable?

Yes, it is. You can go at your own pace. I always meet people where they at, and focus on what they can progressively **leave out** of their lifestyles that is not beneficial for a healthy physiology. We start at the beginning.

For example: If a drug addict stops doing drugs without changing anything else, there will be an improvement in their health. If they stop doing drugs and smoking cigarettes, the improvement will be greater. If they are overeating animal protein and start to reduce it to a reasonable amount, or eliminate it altogether, there will be another level of improvement.

Again, the benefit comes from what is **left out.** That's why so many diets—Macrobiotic, the Zone, etc— all claim results. The common denominator is that **harmful foods and habits are left out completely. This is what** leads to healing.

However, in many cases, what we do and leave in your lifestyle is far from optimal, which results in less than optimal long-term results. On the other hand, if you replace foods and substances that interfere with a healthy physiology with **Real, Fresh Foods,** which will provide all the nutrients you need, you will be well on your way to Your Healthy Journey.

#3 TASTE

I've never eaten this way & I'm willing to make a commitment but is this going to taste good?

Let's start with an all-raw plant-based lifestyle. A lot of people think it must be repetitious and tasteless. I've been eating a 100% raw food lifestyle for over 50 Years and trust me it's the tastiest food you can find; it might tend to be a little repetitious, but the great thing about it is that you lose your cravings for the foods that harm you.

But if you choose the **Intermediate Level Lifestyle/ Menu,** which does include cooked portions with your meals, as well as fruits and vegetables, this can be made into a gourmet way of eating. You will have a tremendous variety of foods to eat, and the health results that you'll achieve can be so astonishing that people who are not familiar with the system would have difficulty believing it is possible.

The great thing about an all-raw plant-based lifestyle is that you lose your cravings for the foods that harm you

#4 REAL FRESH FOODS

Fred, for over fifty years you've been eating raw fruits, vegetables, nuts, seeds & sprouts. Do I have to be that extreme in order to get healthy?

No, you really don't have to do that, to get healthy. As I mentioned above, fifty years experience has shown me that what works best for the majority of people is the **Intermediate Level Lifestyle/Menu;** it's based on eating real food and leaving out any food that interferes with a healthy physiology. It's approximately 80% alkaline and 20% acid and though it's a lot of raw food, you can include cooked food portions with those meals. There's variety available and, if the food is prepared by a competent cook, it's very appetizing. For some people, it may initially prove difficult to leave out processed and junk food; but when you understand the benefits, you should be able to summon up sufficient motivation.

My goal is to meet people right where they are and show them how this can be done—making this a permanent lifestyle gives you an excellent chance of slowing down the aging process, keeping your body weight ideal, being strong and normalizing your blood chemistry. The key is **leaving out** what harms you and **putting in** foods in their cleanest form. Then your body can rise to the occasion and do fabulous things.

#5 HEALTH & LONGEVITY

Can I live a disease-free life & live to a very healthy old age?

Based on my personal experience of living Your Healthy Journey for over 60 years and my clinical practice, I would say yes this can be done. Although, granted one day we will all leave this physical body, you can lead a life that's relatively disease-free. It is true, the body is a self healing, self-regulating biological machine, but there are too many circumstances over which we have no control—our genetic make-up, the environment, etc. But we can do fantastic things if we let our body do what it has to do.

When you clean up your body it takes fewer calories and nutrients to have more energy. I'm on a low calorie and nutrient dense lifestyle and, as I mentioned earlier, at this point in my life it's definitely working for me. My life is a living experiment—I try to learn from this information all the time. This is how I base all my knowledge, experience, and clinical background.

Although the right lifestyle can help us live longer, the key objective is to live a higher quality life. That's what I'm striving for. If I live to be beyond one hundred, that will just be icing on the cake but right now I really enjoy being with my grandchildren. I cannot guarantee you will live to 120 without experiencing disease. But I can say that you will have the healthiest and longest life that is possible for you, and, what's more, you will obtain a deluge of other blessings.

#6 JUICES

I've heard that fresh vegetable juices are important, but shouldn't we be chewing our whole foods instead of drinking the extracts from these foods?

Fresh vegetable juices *are* very important. Although, they are controversial in some ways because there are people who think that if you do not chew whole foods with their fiber, you are not receiving complete nutrition. They claim that vegetable juices really do not have that much value. My experience has been completely different. I've been using vegetable juices my whole life and I've been working with people clinically for over fifty years and there are so many benefits from drinking fresh vegetable juices. Juices provide many of the vitamins and minerals that we need in a pure, easily assimilated form that create the communication between cells which is needed for healing.

Juices provide many of the vitamins and minerals that we need in a pure, easily assimilated form that create the communication between cells which is needed for healing

#7 I'VE GOT GAS

Will changing my lifestyle effect by bowel movements? I've had gas all my life, and what about constipation?

In most cases, constipation is a lifestyle problem. When you eat processed foods, which have little or no fiber, gas and constipation are frequent side effects.

Though vegetable juices don't have fiber, they are extremely beneficial for constipation. I recently consulted with a woman recovering from gall bladder surgery; she wasn't moving her bowels because of the effects of general anesthesia and I told her to drink some vegetable juice—she went to the bathroom twice the next day.

So juices are very successful in addressing this type of a problem, especially when you also take probiotics, systemic enzymes and digestive enzymes. More fundamentally, however, you need to commit to a lifestyle change, correct the foods that you eat and drink, lower your stress level, and you'll find that your problems will very likely clear up.

When you eat processed foods, which have little or no fiber, gas and constipation are frequent side effects.

#8 WOMEN'S ISSUES: THE BODY KNOWS

Women's issues: their cycles, nutrition during pregnancy, early childhood development, hormonal imbalances, & menopausal changes?

There are so many variables associated with this question, however, I will give this general answer: **your body knows what to do**. When you leave out what's causing your problems, the body then strives for its best chemistry. I have seen many women having problems of the kind; when they change their lifestyle, little by little their body starts to balance itself out and they start to feel well. To the degree that a person conscientiously applies lifestyle changes, combined with following the information provided by their doctor, the body is able to help heal itself. When you adopt a healthy lifestyle that excludes the root causes of illness and discomfort, and if the pathways to recovery are then re-opened, then the body, with its wonderfully integrated system of chemical checks and balances, will bring you naturally and effortlessly to your optimal health.

When you leave out what's causing your problems, the body then strives for its best chemistry.

#9 DOING THE RIGHT THING

Will lifestyle changes affect my cholesterol, thyroid, triglyceride, and blood pressure levels?

Thyroid function is a little bit different than the others. I could never tell a person if they've been on synthyroid for an under-active thyroid for two or three years that cleaning up your lifestyle will clear up the problem, though I have seen people able to reduce the amount of medication for this as well as many other problems.

But as far as cholesterol, triglycerides and blood pressure are concerned, I've very rarely seen a person who had changed their lifestyle in a correct way and did not successfully address these conditions. I couldn't count the number of people that have changed their lifestyle and experienced a reduction in their cholesterol and triglyceride levels and seen their blood pressure return to a healthy, ideal range.

It's your body that does it, not the food. I'm not prescribing food as a cure; but what the correct lifestyle does is to allow your body's inherent healing intelligence that knows exactly what to do, to go right into action. If you do the right thing, the impact is dramatic in terms of your well-being, quality of life, sharpness of thinking, and energy—all of which will continue to an advanced age.

#10 RUN, JUMP, SWIM, CAN I DO THAT?

You told us that you're physically fit—you can run, jump, play sports, and you were born in 1929. Well, I'll be turning fifty and I don't have the same physical abilities. Am I going to get that back when I make lifestyle changes?

If you don't have anything organically or mechanically wrong with you, such as serious heart disease, you have a very good chance at age fifty (which is still relatively young) to get back into a very active lifestyle. If you are basically a healthy person, there are very few limitations for you. When you change your lifestyle, your energy really comes back, your endurance picks up, your skin tone improves—everything improves. I don't try to convince a person that changing their lifestyle is going to turn them into a Mongolian warrior, turn their hair black and give them the libido of a Roman soldier, but it *will* do wonders for them. What I do say is that if you do Your Healthy Journey, correctly you have the potential to open your healing pathways and help prevent most chronic and some acute diseases.

The big failure in our society is that people are responding to the health crisis by merely tweaking their routine. They may be eating a little more salad, taking a reportedly magical supplement, and implementing other cosmetic changes advocated by the media, but this kind of thing doesn't go deep enough. You need to learn to eat correctly, leave out all the processed foods and stimulants that interfere with a healthy chemical physiology, and let the healing force within you do its job.

In the beginning it is not easy, but if you do it in the context of the lifestyle change that I'm speaking of, there is a huge variety of tasty foods because I'm not telling you to go out into the backyard and live off the lawn. The key is to eat **Real Fresh Foods**—organically grown foods if you possibly can—and to exclude processed food completely. If you try the raw food lifestyle and don't feel well, it doesn't mean it doesn't suit you; it means that you need more time to stabilize. You may need more knowledge or somebody to guide you. You might need internal cleansing. So I want to encourage everyone to make a lifestyle change but when you have specific problems, get your rest because you may need to cleanse and this will require your internal energy for detox which is what occurs based on the concept of *what you leave out*.

When you change your lifestyle, your energy really comes back, your endurance picks up, your skin tone improves—everything improves.

THE PRODUCTS

There are living raw foods, lifestyle products, supplements and equipment that I may suggest for people to apply to their daily life while on Your Healthy Journey. They are helpful with the transition and a powerful addition to a healthy lifestyle change. All the categories of supplements listed are of the highest quality and formulated under the standard of a low temperature model so the bioavailability is recognized as a whole food by the body. This naturally supplies the healing pathways. But again, REMEMBER, the main focus and the foundation is WHAT YOU LEAVE OUT and a lifestyle of Plant-Based Dominate, Real, Freshly-Prepared Food. This Lifestyle Approach will open up the miraculous remedial healing capabilities of the human body. Please visit our website at www.anydoubtleaveitout.com or if you have any questions please call us at 914-619-5397.

FRED'S CORE LIFESTYLE PRODUCTS

SYSTEMIC ENZYMES
DIGESTIVE ENZYMES
PROBIOTICS
FRED'S GREENFOOD
OMEGA JUICER
OMEGA BLENDER
FRED'S LIFESTYLE BUNDLES

ENJOY YOUR HEALTHY JOURNEY!!

THE PLACE

Most times you will be preparing your meals in your own kitchen but there are more and more places opening up that are preparing raw food meals & raw juices. I go to many raw food restaurants and some follow healthy practices and some miss the mark, so be aware, where you eat, but if you in New York City, I recommend and have eaten at the Juice Press. I know they use quality certified organic foods and follow the principles of Your Healthy Journey!

Your Healthy Journey Experiences

Dr Fred Bisci has been my friend and mentor for a substantial part of my life, and he is the person who has had the most positive impact on me. In order to achieve ultimate health, and as a means for cleansing one's mind, body and soul, Fred's new book is a "must read".

Vincent J. Gallo, attorney

Fred Bisci is the Master of Health... A man who walks his talk... Fred has proven to me time and time again that Your Healthy Journey is a living adventure; it's not a fad or a diet, it's a lifestyle that proves that anything is possible through making the right choices and healthy living.

Diamond Dallas Page, ex-professional wrestler /YRG Fitness System

I have always been impressed by Dr. Fred Bisci's extraordinary compassion and knowledge. He is one of the finest people I know and I welcome this opportunity to tell the world! People who know Dr. Bisci have been telling him for years to share his knowledge and extensive experience about nutrition and health in a book and finally it is here. This is a great opportunity to share Dr. Bisci's wealth of information for your benefit and possibly to help others.

David Norman, real estate Developer Founder

I weighed 297 pounds when Diamond Dallas Page, creator of YRG, sent me Dr Fred Bisci's Intermediate Level plan. I followed it and I lost over 30 pounds in the first month, 100 pounds in the first six months, and I eventually reached 156 pounds! Dr Bisci's plan is not about dieting; it is about eating clean wholesome food. I can and will follow this healthy eating plan for the rest of my life.

Arthur Boorman, school teacher

In this landmark book, Dr. Fred Bisci's wisdom is practical, readable, and yet challenging. He is an encouraging guide as you weave your way along Your Healthy Journey

Daniel Pender, Family therapist

Dr. Fred Bisci is one in a million. His professionalism and dedication to the field of medically-based nutrition, complemented by a holistic approach to total well-being, has set the standard for health professionals. Moreover, Dr. Bisci walks his talk by living a lifestyle demonstrative of the very principles he teaches to his clients and patients. 'Your Healthy Journey' is a genuine, well-founded resource that provides the necessary tools for 'Discovering your body's full potential'.

William J. Smith MS,PHD, triathlon athlete

Dr. Fred Bisci has taught me to choose foods that give me sustainable energy that meets the demands of my lifestyle as a wife, mother and psychotherapist. Now that I am preparing and eating whole & raw foods, my health has improved dramatically, my energy level has increased and I am inspiring friends, family, and patients. At the age of 51, I am now living my life!

Denise a. Wind, RDH, LCSW—Psychotherapist

Fred reminds me of Brando in the Godfather movie because he has the same innate, deep understanding of each person that comes to him and of their problem. He listens to their complaints and then immediately springs into action, drawing on his years of experience to dispense words of reassurance, reality, comfort, wisdom, and knowledge. Simply put, Fred is the Godfather of nutrition!

Joseph Serpico, Personal Friend

Intelligence, humility, intuition, generosity and kindness. These are just a few of the words that describe my friend and mentor, Dr. Fred Bisci. I have traveled the world and met many other wonderful and gifted people, but there are few who can match Dr. Bisci's unique melding of knowledge of the human body, application of effective and natural remedies, and a genuine willingness to help.

Peter A. Cervoni/vegan & raw food Chef

I share the view of many people who believe that Dr Fred Bisci is the world's foremost nutritional scientist! His Intermediate Level Lifestyle has given me an allergy free-energy filled life compatible with spirituality and emotional well being. His writings can truly bring a revolution in the health industry for all people!

Bishop Joseph Mattera

I have personally consulted with Fred on several occasions regarding personal situations about my health. I have found that Fred made an intensive inquiry regarding my nutrition and the detail of my condition. He has made several suggestions and specific recommendations that he believed would be beneficial to me. What stands out in my mind is his thoroughness and broad Spectrum analysis through his questioning.

Walter J. Urban, Ph.D. Psychoanalyst/ "Do You Have the courage to change"

Dr. Fred Bisci has been on the cutting edge of natural health and the raw food movement for more than 50 years. He is undeniably one of the most knowledgeable people in the field of natural health. No one I know digs deeper and researches each topic more thoroughly than Dr. Bisci. He shows absolutely no bias in drawing his conclusions. Without doubt, he is a sincere truth seeker!

Bob Mccauley, Certified Taekwondo Instructor/Master Herbalist

"Fred changed my life. His genius and vast knowledge of the body relative to health is daunting. He's helped me and countless friends and relatives of mine. I treasure his advice!

Susan Tully & Ray Klas/ interior Designers

Over the years I have heard a mantra continuously spoken within the circle of people that have been privileged to sit in Dr. Bisci's office or that have heard him speak to an audience. "Does he have a book? When is his book coming out?" The moment you feel the power of his intellect and the sincerity of his intentions you immediately want more. It has taken many years for this book to come to fruition for one main reason because for over fifty years Dr. Bisci has fully given his attention to the people he has been helping. This selfless commitment to his clients has finally come together in this book as the most valuable, groundbreaking approach to overcoming and preventing disease. Fred Bisci, born 1929, is a living testament to the validity of his program. Dr. Bisci's life experience is a gift to all of us, practitioners, clients and anyone who is willing and open to the power of this lifestyle.

ENJOY YOUR HEALTHY JOURNEY!

Michael Perrine/Colonic Hydrotherapist & Detoxification consultant

Where do I begin to tell you about the miracles of the "Fred Bisci Lifestyle"? How fortunate I am to have Fred as my brother-in-law. Twenty years ago I was in a serious car accident that required over 200 stitches above my right eye and I also had 5 broken bones in my left hand and wrist.

While in the hospital Fred told me that he could help me recuperate faster by changing the way that I ate. A while back, when I was a professional basketball player in my 20's, Fred was always telling me how he could make me a better athlete by changing my eating and drinking lifestyle, but I didn't believe him. So after the accident I was desperate and ready to try anything. So after three days in the hospital, I returned home to start Fred's lifestyle. Before every meal I would have a 12 to 16 oz glass of carrot, celery and apple juice. My breakfast would consist of a variety of fresh fruits, not out of a can or processed. For lunch I would have my juice followed by a large vegetable salad with extra virgin olive oil, a lemon or raw apple cider vinegar. For dinner I would have my juice, a nice sized salad, steamed vegetables and a small piece of chicken breast or fish.

*Fred informed me that the most important thing was not what I ate **but what I left out**. There were no more chips, pizza, fried foods, beef or pork, white rice or white pasta and desserts smothered with sugar; only fresh, natural, healthy foods. I stayed with the plan and 10 days after the accident I returned to the hospital to have my hand examined. There must have been 200 people waiting to see these 10 hand doctors at Belleview Hospital in New York. When my doctor examined me he asked me if I would move my fingers very slowly. He said it would hurt but I had to start getting movement in my fingers. When I moved my fingers it was as if I was playing a piano, he was so amazed that he called the other nine doctors into his cubicle to explain what a fabulous job he did operating on my hand, and once again in front of the other Doctors he asked me to move my fingers. When I moved them effortlessly, all of the Doctors were flabbergasted. That is when I really became a believer in Fred and his lifestyle change program.*

Since that time I have introduced many professional athletes to Fred Bisci and he has helped them tremendously with enhancing their athletic careers. I have also had the opportunity to see Fred help countless others who had serious life threatening ailments and are now running marathons and triathlons.

I have made Fred's lifestyle approach a part of the mind, body and soul training regimen that I preach to big time athletes as well as the youth. What you leave out and then what you put in is the key to a healthy lifestyle. Thanks Fred for enlightening me so much and May God Bless You.

Ralph Menar, President Dream Sports & Entertainment

My father has been using the services of Dr. Bisci for almost one year in an attempt to reduce the symptoms of Parkinson's Disease. Dr. Bisci placed my father on a lifestyle designed to detoxify his body of impurities. This lifestyle eliminated dairy products, red meat, and alcohol, and relies on vegetables, fruits, and freshly squeezed vegetables juices. Since starting this lifestyle my father has lost weight, he is more alert, and he is more energetic. The trembling of his hands as well as other associated symptoms of Parkinson's Disease has dramatically diminished. Even his eyes, which were yellowish in color, have become clear. It appears that my father has benefited and continues to benefit from Dr. Bisci's expertise in the field of nutritional healing. We Thank you.

Dr. Louise Priolo MD

"Dr. Bisci is the most learned nutritionist I know. His vast knowledge of the human organism, optimal lifestyle and living the life of Real, Fresh Foods is unparalleled. What separates Dr. Bisci from his peers is that he has lived on a completely raw food lifestyle longer than anyone else I know. His journey was one of transformation from a meat eating bodybuilder to inviting people to experience this mostly raw food life. His gift is meeting people where there at, when there're ready to make a lifestyle change. Fred helped me in healing my own affliction by setting up a lifestyle that was comprehensive. Not only is he my nutritionist but it is a privilege to call him my friend."

John Sands, Music Director, IMg Media Group

On a professional level Dr. Bisci increased the efficacy of my treatments by counseling me with natural remedies for pain and inflammation. On a personal level he changed my life. Every day I feel how my overall health has improved because of Dr. Bisci's approach and lifestyle instruction. He continues to change the face of nutrition and does it in a way that is easy to implement and follow. If you want to take control of your health and free yourself from the perils of degenerative conditions, than do what I do, and abide by every word.

Joseph M Dimino, MSPT, Dimino Physical therapy

I met Fred Bisci when I was 15 years old. I was working as a stock boy in a Health Food store in Staten Island, NY. Fred was the consulting nutritionist at the time. What a remarkable man! His knowledge and wisdom is second to none in the healthcare/nutrition field. Combined with his core values and spirituality Fred is truly a luminary in the field of nutrition, healthcare, and well being. One of the greatest men I have ever met.

Dr. Bill Busch/Dentist

Dr. Bisci is a living example of the importance of understanding the body's ability to heal. His years of researching the intricacies of the body has lent to the development of a program that goes beyond counting calories and gets to the heart of true health by taking nutrition and combining it with the psychological and spiritual aspects. I was able to learn firsthand, the impact of his work through my own healing experience with breast cancer. Utilizing the guidelines detailed within this book, he has provided me with a tool box for becoming my own best advocate for healthy living. This book is a must read for those of you looking for a transformational experience.

Clarisse M. Domingo ICSW, CHHC, Founder of Journey Back to Health

I came to Fred 3 years ago to help solve a stomach condition, allergy to fruit, and overall health problems. I wanted to feel good all of the time and not be sluggish any more. My wife joined me in this quest and we have never felt better.

As commissioner of parks for Nassau County I am faced with many demands that require my full attention and more importantly my ability to think on my feet as a situation arises. I am also a professional triathlete. Eating this way allows me to be on my game every day with no regret and have better performance to the best of my ability. I couldn't imagine my life any other way than the way it is now...eating clean, fresh, organic food adapted to my individual body.

Jose Lopez/Nassau county Parks Commissioner, elite triathlon, US World team

Rory Dean, DC. (born 1957)
Decade long Fred Bisci buddy and associate.
The human body was created
to stay healthy for all people,
for all time who face the practice,
openly, everyday.

"ENJOY YOUR HEALTHY JOUREY"

Freddy's Thoughts:

"What You Leave Out is the Foundation"

I am not sure if people really understand the importance of "What You Leave Out." Because the concept, once you really look at it, I say it's pretty profound. This is the real basis and commitment for Your Healthy Journey

"Water Fasting"

Water fasting is based on the concept of "What You Leave Out" where you're leaving out everything accept water. This will create a reciprocal amount of improvement until you go too far and your body is not really fasting anymore. So when your water fasting we have to realize that there is going to be a tremendous change in your body's chemistry and the detox will be very, very dramatic. This is why this should really be done, under supervision.

I have had many personal experiences from water fasting and what I found out, was the more you did it, the more you understood profoundly what was happening, emotionally, mentally, physically and spiritually, if it was done correctly.

When you're water fasting you're leaving out all the processed foods (cake, candy, ice cream, soda, bread, pasta, pizza, etc.) and stimulants (alcohol, smoking, caffeine, refined sugar, meat, etc.) that are counter-indicated for a healthy physiology. So what happens when you do this? Well the body goes into a remedial mode where it starts to cleanse your body and after a certain period of time, it starts to live off the endogenous waste that's in your cells (digestive, muscular, joints, circulatory, organ cellular systems).

One mistake that I see people do while they're water fasting is that they run all over the place and they say they feeling really good. Yes this does happen. Although there are people out there who were very active during very long heroic fasts, from my experience, this is not the correct way to do it. The best way and first thing to do is to work with someone who is a fasting expert and the main key is to do it as an emotional, mental, physical and spiritual level, rest period. If you do it this way you can regenerate cells and the effects are incredible. The simple way to do this is drink water, rest and close your eyes as much as possible because when your eyes are open you are expending another 40% of your energy to your brain to evaluate what your seeing. This 40% is then being taking away from your vital energy for detox and regeneration. I realized this as I was doing my second 40 day water fast where I rested completely on all levels and could go twice as long and only lose ½ pound a day instead of the one pound a day. Even though I learned a lot about water fasting I do not recommend long water fasting anymore but if you decide to do it, I would say no longer then 21 days. That's if you are resting on all levels and under supervision.

Now, don't get me wrong there are people who are on record that have done a long fast, like Dick Gregory. What he did under medical supervision was 70 days of water fasting and then broke the fast on a glass of orange juice and actually ran and walked 100 miles. This has been documented. So all these people that say you cannot do feats of strength and endurance without an adequate amount of animal protein have to realize that it can be done because that's what Dick Gregory, Barbara Moore and I have experienced.

I remember when I was challenged by a person at a health food store to run after water fasting. I realized that I could do it because I had the experience, understood resting on all levels, was overall efficient and was not strained from the detox process. So I did a 10 day water fast, rested most of the time and closed my eyes as much as possible. So when the word got out, on the day of the run, a big crowd, cameras and spectators showed up. That really wasn't what I was looking for because I just looked at this as a personal challenge to see if I could really do it.

So after my 10 day water fast, I run 10 miles and it was easy. Although I was thin to begin with, someone took a picture of me and it was not flattering but I really felt strong. This was another example that led me to the importance of "What You Leave Out" and how this could be done in the context of longevity and a healthy lifestyle. This is my mainstream approach of the Intermediate Level Lifestyle.

Of course, I don't recommend that anybody try what I did because all of this is for information only.

"Juice Fasting"

I would recommend that instead of water fasting that people do (vegetable/green) juice fasting. Now many people have gone on long juice fasts from 60-90 days. Dick Gregory lived on juices for a year and I lived on juices for months at a time. It's not a big deal.

Again when you're on juices you're leaving everything out. So in spite if people think you're starving yourself, realize other people and cultures, for periods of time, have lived a healthy life without the necessity for solid food or animal protein. This can be erroneous on the surface because when people have been eating a lot of animal protein try to do juice fasting they will fall flat on their face. We just have to keep in mind that there's a major chemistry shift that you have to adjust to when you go on a juice fast. Also, above and beyond people eating too much animal protein, people can eat too much protein from a vegetarian source. Anything, that promotes unnatural growth no matter how good you think you look, like 18 inch arms and a 50 inch chest, will require you to over nourish yourself to maintain it. This is just not healthy. Although it might be good for your ego it is not good for your longevity. It's that simple!

I have seen plenty of people that have enormous physiques that over nourish themselves with 5-6 meals a day and when they try to reduce it, they get dizzy and light-headed and they are told its hypoglycemia. This is not hypoglycemia; it's just the body trying to clean out and restore itself to a healthy equilibrium from the reduction of animal protein. Others may tell you that you are not getting enough animal protein when you get weak, it's just not true. What makes it not true is that people over time in other nations have lived their lives without animal protein and they have better health and longevity.

I myself, can go days without eating solid food and feel relatively the same as when as I was eating. So you don't need the over nourishment that some people think they need. You just need the nutrients in the right way.

So when you go on (vegetable/green) juices you should

drink a variety of juices. Also be aware there are juice programs and stories out there where people have lost 50-100 pounds. So be prudent about what you do because traditionally people say it's very dangerous but it's not, if you work with someone who is experienced. Also this is not recommended when you on a lot of medication, have emotional or psychological problems and don't understand what's happening. Plus anybody that has a lot of fears and anxiety should not do water fasting and maybe shouldn't go on a juice fast. So get supervision so you are not misinterpreting what's happening.

"Food Fast"

Then the next level is what I call the food fast. This is where people are eating just fruits, vegetables, juices, salads and simple smoothies without nuts and seeds. You can go on for months on this lifestyle. It's really amazing how long you can go. Again you're leaving out all the processed foods and stimulants plus the grains, nuts and seeds. When you do this correctly you will end up going into a detox that's a little slower then water or even juice fasting.

Now, remember that everything you leave out will give you a reciprocal amount of improvement and when I say that there is going to be improvement that doesn't mean right from the get go. Initially you will probably go into a detox where you will feel poor in health but this will eventually lead you to improvement. We just have to understand detox is a process that is ongoing to different degrees. People need to identify with this!

The symptoms of detox are one in the same as the problems you have presently or from your past. What really happens when you go through a detox is the release of these endogenous materials from the cells. This will affect you in your weaken and overburdened areas, where your having the problem but eventually you go through the detox and start to regenerate the cells, if you do this right.

For instance, if you have previous injuries or have an arthritic condition and go on a juice fast or food fast, you're going to feel it more in that area. I had a serious shoulder injury from a car accident and when a detox is going on for me, that's the first place I feel it.

We have to get a clearer picture because there is so much confusion. Some people have such radical approaches to change that are just not compliant. Most people don't want to do water fasting, maybe not even a juice fast or an all raw food lifestyle. Some people don't want to become vegans. So I prefer people to go to my Intermediate Level Lifestyle where I can encourage you to become a vegan, if you want. You can also eat a moderate amount of animal protein, if desired, because if you do decide to eat some clean animal protein (without hormones or antibiotics, grass-fed) you can still be healthy. This is possible!

This is where the radical approaches make the mistake. Everybody that forms a radical program is based on their experience and the science they have been exposed to. I not a dogmatic person and have seen thousands and thousands of people and everybody that comes to see me wants to do something healthy but they don't want to do the same thing. It would be so easy to just have people go on a vegan or raw food lifestyle if they can but there's an option. If people can stay within the Intermediate Level Lifestyle parameters (leaving out all the processed foods) a person can live and achieve better health. The Intermediate Level Lifestyle works extremely well. I have seen some miraculous recoveries and changes in people very quickly.

"Processed Food"

I have said this before but processed food is a modern day curse. With the advent of processed foods after World War II, we have developed many more diseases then if we had omitted processed food. When you leave out processed food, chronic disease should not develop to that state in the body as it is today because the body's remedial process is there to keep us healthy. Of course if you ask most medical doctors they might not agree with this but I have watched plenty of people, from my 50 years of experience that eliminated all processed foods that had chronic and some acute conditions that lived within the Intermediate Level Lifestyle that were successful. This is not a radical approach for people, if you want to change and stay with it the rest of your life.

"Reciprocal Improvement and Reciprocal Deterioration"

Now there's a reciprocal amount of improvement from what you leave out and the freshly prepared foods within the Intermediate Level Lifestyle that is conducive to a healthy physiology. There's also a reciprocal amount of deterioration to the cellular tissue from what we're doing when we're eating foods that are harmful. The poor quality, over nourishment and amounts of food that people are eating today will cause this deterioration. Unfortunately the standard American diet is a disaster; most people eating that type of diet are just surviving on their genetic makeup. Of course, if they have good genes they are going to last longer but a lot of people are losing their quality of life at a much younger age. There are a lot of people walking around that seem like their healthy but end up on medication. They are in the ongoing process of developing clinical diseases. But if they were following a healthy lifestyle this may not have happened. The reality that people are living a long life but it's not a **quality long life**. Most people are living with conditions that are depriving them the joy of a vibrant healthy life up until an advanced age. Yes, there are more factors and variables associated with what you eat or drink but it is important that people start a lifestyle change with the elimination of processed foods and get into a lifestyle that is conducive to them individually to attain their goals.

"Water"

Drinking water is important because it's a solvent and a transport medium. Water helps dissolve and remove endogenous materials from our body. I know of a medical doctor that boasts that he never had a glass of water in 40 years and that water is a waste of time for him. Well, I have never heard of anything so ridiculous in my life.

"Writing Books and Making Statements"

We have to remember there are many people out there making statements and writing books that seem to be well qualified but are incorrect based on the misinterpretation of their/the experience. We're also told by some medical professionals and scientists that what you eat or drink really doesn't make much of a difference in your recovery. Well I think that people making statements like that are surely misinformed and they are doing a lot of damage to the people they suppose to be helping.

"Capitalistic Health System"

We must understand this is a capitalistic system. People are motivated by monetary gain. Unfortunately that is the predominating factor in our so-called health system.

Our healthcare system in my opinion could be fantastic but in reality it's incomplete and drives people to failure. The information that mainstream healthcare is providing is mostly inaccurate. Now, there are times when people may need medical attention or surgery when there is a life threatening situation going on in order to save their life but what I am saying is that the system of prevention in this country is misleading and incorrect. People should be told that our current lifestyles lead to 85% of our diseases. 85% of our diseases come from what we knowingly and unknowing put into our mouths, breathe into our lungs or touches our skin. It's that simple. If we have a good idea of what prevention really is this will help us from getting these chronic degenerative diseases. Please be watchful of those that are only motivated to make the all mighty dollar!

"Our Mouths, Our Lungs, Our Skin"

I believe that the majority of our diseases enter our body through our mouth, our lungs, and our skin. My theory is that the problems in this day and age commence in our GI tract. I believe that most people do not realize how much harm they are doing when they push food or whatever is disguised as food by processing into their mouth. One of the problems that I see frequently is constipation and bowel function. I have known thousands of people that move their bowels only twice a week and were told that was normal by their doctor. I believe that to be incorrect and a precursor to disease. What you eat today should come out of you tomorrow; one time for each meal that you eat. When food stays inside of your GI tract too long you can end up with a problem. This could be more serious than the average person might understand.

I also believe we are making a tremendous mistake concerning the nature of many of our diseases. Science and research keeps focusing on treating the symptoms of people's problems rather than the cause. Research keeps quoting double blind studies that turn into scientific information, than after couple of years it turns out to be abstract, half true or completely flawed. I am not a big fan or a believer of double blind studies. I personally believe that they are not only confusing the average person but also many of our scientists. It is very easy to be misled by fancy medical terminology and labeling that comes along with research. The bottom line, to me is "Why aren't we resolving our health problems?" We seem to be in limbo because what is right today, new research makes it wrong tomorrow. This just leads to more confusion.

I don't think there is one field where there is more confusion than in the field of health, nutrition, and how to lead a healthy lifestyle. There is no doubt that we have great medical and scientific minds that are doing wonderful things in their field and yet we have not really determined many of our health issues. I believe the medical profession should be spending more time in educating people on how to prevent disease by living the right lifestyle. I believe that the food giants are taking healthy food, processing it and sooner or later it will make us sick. From that point, people go to medication and surgery and are caught up in what I believe to be a vicious cycle.

I believe that your upper GI tract in some respects is like a second brain. What goes through your GI tract is giving your life, giving you disease or shorting your lifespan. I also believe this process is putting your chemistry under a tremendous burden and the end result is causing inflammation, sickness and depriving you of oxygen on a cellular level. I believe it is critically important that we eliminate the processed food completely because it is making the body an inefficient biological organism. You must clean up your body so you can properly utilize oxygen from your lungs and absorb the proper nutrition. I personally believe that we need a new approach to cancer research.

My personal thoughts are that we need a new answer to cancer and the nature of our diseases. People in general are following lifestyles that will make them better **HOSTS** for not only infectious diseases but also most of our chronic diseases. I believe that people are more confused than ever. Every month some new book comes out that is just another confusing contradiction.   This is not helping people. Much of the information is recycled, misleading or promotional hype. Of course there are many good books available and because of expediential technology that is available on the internet we have to separate the truth from what might not be. My advice is whether you have a problem or not because of what's happening in this day and age, to consider a lifestyle change like Your Healthy Journey. Diets don't work and they probably never will. Remember a lifestyle change done correctly will give you a very good chance of preventing disease. Keep in mind, that I would not follow the advice of anyone that tells you it is too hard, it can't be done or why deprive yourself when you take pleasure in your life.

If you are willing to help yourself you can be successful. There are no absolutes but many things are obviously better than others. My opinion is that most of our problems begin in our upper GI tract which is 16 to 20 feet of the looped small intestine. When food is consumed late at night or highly processed or stays too long in our upper GI tract it's not normal and it will cause problems. No matter what you eat, be protein or starch, it will not digest properly and probable ferment. This will become like a sewer gas which is very acid forming and will deprive you the ability of getting oxygen efficiently to the lungs and cells. This lack of efficient oxygen exchange will cause more endogenous materials to build up anywhere in your body. This leads to ongoing irritation, inflammation and insufficiency. So when oxygen is taken into the lungs this inefficiency will cause difficulty and dysfunction with cells and organs which will affect your performance. I have seen many people that have COPD, chronic breathing problems or with no endurance, change their lifestyle and be able to run and bound up a flight of stairs over time.

Now this fermentation process that I'm talking about does not necessarily have to come from sugar and I certainly do not believe that people should avoid fresh organically grown fruits and vegetables in the right amounts. Avoiding fruits is misleading.

I run into many people that have stopped eating fruit because of the information they are seeing on the internet or from some books. Also, I think this occurred from what Otto Warburg, Nobel Peace Prize Laureate, said ("that cancer is caused by lack of oxygen and thrives on fermentative non-oxidative respiration") and is being taken out of context and misunderstood. This fermentative non-oxidative process could take place from incomplete combustion and indigestion of any food that is not being broken down and moved through your system rapidly enough. Remember everything we eat is converted to glucose and the normal blood sugar range is between 70 and 99 generally. If you are not a diabetic, no matter what you're eating, your body will keep you in that range through homeostasis but remember it will catch up with you if you are eating anything you want.

Also if what some people are saying about fruits and vegetables is true, including some scientists, than a person that eats mostly animal protein with no fruits and vegetables, would not be getting cancer. This is definitely not true and is a very controversial debate.

We always must try to get the best health advice and information on lifestyle changes to try to correct the causes of our problems. That's why I believe lifestyle changes are imperative for anybody that has any disease. This is true concerning cancer. You must be determined to be responsible for our own health and be free to make the right choices. Over eating, layering food on top of food, eating too frequently and eating too late at night, not only accelerates our aging process but is a major factor in the development of any disease. When our GI tract is fermenting and off-gassing, it's diffusing into our blood to our cells. This is depriving us of many essential nutrients and oxygen that your body needs to remain healthy. My belief is that the upper GI tract is the root cause of cancer and a clean GI tract allows the fresh air exchange into our lungs and the proper functioning of our skin, which is critical. There are over 10,000 chemicals that are going into our bodies and we need to have a good working oxygen exchange system which helps in proper elimination. This inefficient process is a major part of the problem, what we eat and what we breathe is what clogs us up and could eventually poison us. Let's get responsible, seek information for good decisions and make a commitment to Your Healthy Journey.

"Holistic Medicine and Anti-Aging"

There is so much hype about holistic medicine and anti-aging.

There's so much talk about HGH, testosterone and bio-identical hormones. I believe people are investing in this new research because there looking for a panacea where they don't have to be responsible for their own health. Now, the newest and latest attraction is stem cells which have a lot of validity but again it is becoming more commercially abstract then real. What I have seen in my life and practice is that people are looking for more ways to look well and slowing down their aging process without taking responsibility on a daily basis to practice and follow a correct healthy lifestyle. Both men and women are using HGH, testosterone and bio-identical hormones for anti-aging. Well I'm not saying that it is totally invalid but that's not something I would encourage people to do because I have seen some people run into real problems. I believe the right way to slow down your aging process far better than the magic bullets of HGH, testosterone and bio-identical hormones is to change your lifestyle by leaving out the processed foods, not eating late at night and reducing the amount of food that you eat where you're completely nourished. Overeating and eating late at night is a sure fire way to accelerate your aging process and get old looking fast. This is a proven fact but there is just no money in telling people to give up processed foods, eat lots of raw food, minimize your animal protein or avoid it completely. But I will tell you that this is the ultimate way to slow down the aging process. If you do this correctly you should be vital and alive up into your 100's. I am working on doing that right now going into my ninth decade being born in 1929. In spite of severe injuries in my life, I still train every day. I do martial arts, Chi Gong, Pilates, Yoga, dumbbells and calisthenics. I want to enjoy a healthy life and do what I want to do if possible all of my life. So should you if you want to!

"Climatic Conditions"

Most people don't understand how climatic conditions or daylight and darkness can affect you health when you on Your Healthy Journey or life in general. People will ask me what that has to do with my lifestyle. Well it has a lot to do with it. Climatic conditions have a tremendous influence on your body's biochemistry. In other words, when you're eating a raw food lifestyle or a vegan lifestyle and you live in the tropics like Florida, Southern California or Costa Rica it will be much easier then living this lifestyle in colder climates like Alaska, New York winters or Canada. There is a tremendous difference. Also if you are living this lifestyle incorrectly in a colder climate and you don't understand your nutrient needs, you will not last or fail completely.

Climatic conditions have such an influence on what we're doing that's why certain cultures tell you to eat the food that is indigenous to the area. The reason they tell you this is that the food that is available naturally is more compatible with the climate you're living in.

For instance, in the tropics they have fruit trees and lots of vegetation. In very cold climates where there is not a lot of vegetation, they eat more concentrated foods which are more compatible with their body's biochemistry for that area. Now, it doesn't mean it's healthier but what I am saying for example is that the Eskimos who have very little vegetation can essentially live on whale blubber, fish and seal meat. In spite of that diet, as a group, Eskimos have a low incidence of coronary heart disease but they have other problems. They don't live as long but we have to factor what's going for them; the air is clean, the whale blubber, fish and seal meat is organic and they're getting clean water. So these people can do ok, not because of the limitations on their diet but because the traditional Eskimo is leaving out all the processed foods and chemicals which we in the states are literally bathing in. Part of this bathing comes from air and water pollution from our cars, carpets, products, and from manufacturing and energy plant smokestacks.

Combine this with antibiotics and hormones in our animals and the chemicals in processed food which festers inside us which our body has to deal with. All these things are what burdens the body, genetically expresses our weaknesses and will make us potential sick.

Alternatively when you're living in a tropical environment on a raw food lifestyle where there are fruits, vegetables and sprouts, you can really live well on a plant-based lifestyle and you don't need a lot of calories. If you do this right you don't even need a lot of concentrated foods. The reason for this is that the climate provides direct energy from the sun to energize your body, increase nutrient absorption and keep you warm. It takes a lot of internal energy output to keep you warm in cold weather. We also have to remember that raw food is very cooling. That is why with high temperatures you will not even break a sweat especially if you are very efficient but the same person living in a cold climate will need more calories to keep their body working efficiently. This is so your body doesn't have to work hard to bring you to normal temperature but keep in mind, if you're comfortable and your temperature is lower than normal, you will live a lot longer.

There is also a so-called advantage with climatic conditions when you're eating a moderate amount of cooked portions with your meals in a cold climate. It will create radiant heat within the body and not tax your body or deprive you of your energy. It will bring up your basal metabolism and keep you warm. Also another way to compensate for the cold temperature is to wear warm layered clothing.

Remember a raw food lifestyle has to be done in an individual way whether you are in a warm and especially cold climate. I have experienced some real cold winters in New York and we have to realize that there are adjustments we have to make during that period. This is another reason why I created the Intermediate Level Lifestyle because there is a versatility that you can do within Your Healthy Journey to respond to the change in seasons. It allows you to go from the cold climate and change gradually when the warm weather approaches.

So when you living the Intermediate Level Lifestyle, you're eating mostly raw foods in the warm weather and when it starts to get cold you can eat some more concentrated foods, sprouts and consume little more calories when needed, plus you can eat some cooked portions with your meals. When you're in warm weather you change back to eating more fruits, vegetables, drinking juices and having blended smoothies while decreasing the cooked portions of your meal.

There is just no problem going from season to season as long as you are staying within the Intermediate Level Lifestyle. Balance in the cells is important with the seasons, cold weather contracts them and warm weather relaxes them. This homeostasis keeps us healthy.

Also utilization of the sun's energy is extremely useful for your health. Exercising outdoors, near the ocean for the negative ions or around trees for the oxygen exchange is so valuable. This is a great way to get electromagnetically grounded. Some people don't realize that it's happening but it really is and it's healthy. So do it and experience this natural God-giving, unconditional gift.

"Daylight and Darkness Theory"

We have to realize that there are changes that take place in the body when we go from daylight to darkness and back again. Please hear this with an open mind. When it goes from daylight to darkness and your eyes dilate this sends a message to your optic nerve that will communicate to your brain a signal to your hypothalamus gland. At this point it will start to slow down your metabolism and give you the ability to get ready to replenish yourself through sleep. So when the next daylight occurs whether it's the morning sun or the middle of the afternoon you should feel refreshed, from a good's night's sleep the night before.

It is just so important to get a good night's sleep because it affects people on all levels of their life. This is why I encourage people not to eat late at night or before you go to bed because your metabolism is not at peak efficiency to breakdown your food properly. When you eat late at night, you are accelerating your aging process and you're creating a lot of endogenous waste in the system which will deposit in your cells. If you keep doing it, it will make you sick. There's no two ways about it, it's a factor in degenerative disease and you will not get a good night's sleep!

Surprisingly, people that do to bed on an empty stomach, in spite of their diet and eat 1-2 small meals a day can live beyond 100 years of age. I met someone like that in my neighborhood named Luigi. I was very impressed when I saw this man. He moved around like a young person. He had a huge head of gray hair, a full set of teeth in his mouth and he told me he walked every day. I really thought the man was in his sixties or younger but when he told me his real age which was 104 years old, I almost fell over because he definitely didn't look it.

Of course I asked him what he ate. The first thing he told me is he didn't like meat and didn't eat it. He said likes fresh homemade soup, vegetables, a glass of wine every once and a while and on rare occasions had a little sheep cheese. Now the big question I had to ask him was how many times a day do you eat. He said in Italian, Uno one meal a day. Now the average doctor would think that Luigi wasn't getting enough to eat but trust me he looked healthier than some 20-40 year olds walking around. Now Luigi really didn't know anything about nutrition per say, he just did it naturally. Although, I've lost contact with him because I think he went back to Italy, I hope and pray that Luigi, who is a fine gentleman and had a great handle on the realities of life is alive and still doing well.

Another story I want to tell you is about how I realized that overeating and eating late at night is not good for you. I remember when I was young when I first started eating raw food; I was a heavy muscled 200 pounder. In the beginning, I was losing a tremendous amount of weight and the more I ate the more my body weight kept staying lower and lower. I came to realize, it was because I was overeating frequently on large salads and eating late at night. Now I really thought this would help me gain weight but instead I was actually losing weight. Not only did this not feel good but I was actually losing more weight because of fermentation, improper digestion and depriving oxygen to my cells. This was just another reason to understand the importance of daylight and darkness and how it relates to living a healthy lifestyle. This personal experience showed me another lesson for Your Healthy Journey so I can show you.

So the point about getting a good night's sleep is to go to bed on an empty stomach and don't eat late at night because the most important sleep that takes place is between 10pm-2am. This is the anabolic stage where the body is going through cell detoxification and regeneration of new cells. So it's really imperative that we understand because when you do it right, you going to wake up fully refreshed and ready for your day.

Now the reverse can take place in the morning with your metabolism. When you're getting up early and you're eating a big, heavy breakfast you're making the same mistake as eating late at night. This could almost be more harmful then going to bed with food in your stomach because your metabolism in the early morning is at a complete standstill and operating very slowly. To literally dump food in your stomach at that point is a disaster. So the best way to do this, if you wake up early is to do some exercise to bring your metabolic rate up to speed and afterward consume something lite like juices or a small amount of fruit. But in reality you really don't have to eat till late morning if you doing this right.

One thing I would also like to specifically comment on is that I don't recommend that you eat a high protein breakfast in the morning. People that make those statements are just stimulating your body and don't understand the human biochemistry and physiology for health and longevity.

Also people must also understand the influence of the moon and the sun which has a tremendous influence on the body's lymphatic system and how it's relates to our

Circadian Rhythms. Circadian rhythms are physical, mental and behavioral changes that follow a roughly 24-hour cycle, within the body, responding primarily to light and darkness in an organism's environment. They are found in most living things, including humans, animals, plants and many tiny microbes. Circadian rhythms control the ebb and flow of our body's biochemistry.

If you really want to slow down your aging process you have to plug into understanding climatic conditions, daylight and darkness and how anabolism is affected when you're going through a restful sleep cycle. This is very important. If you do this you may never need to take HGH, testosterone or bio-identical hormones. Although when people are following an incorrect lifestyle they will eventually burnout and may start using HGH, testosterone or bio-identical hormones in place of following a good lifestyle. So I believe that living Your Healthy Journey is a better way to do it so there is no potential for burnout.

Please remember none of us are going to live forever but we should all want to slow down our aging process if we want to or if we can. The key is to respect your Circadian rhythms, keep a balanced cycle and stay consistent.

"Common Denominator and Diet Books"

Bringing it full circle, there are many dietary lifestyles that are not optimal that may seem to work not because of what the person is ingesting but from "What You Leave Out." "What You Leave Out" will always help you have better odds with the prevention of degenerative diseases. This is why I am so animate with people to understand the concept of "What You Leave Out." It's a life saver and it is the most important thing to understand!

That's why there are so many diet books out there that work for each author. It's mainly from "What You Leave Out." This is the common denominator because these books are always leaving out what's harmful like processed food. The human body has outstanding adaptive abilities if you are feeding it real food that is fresh and unprocessed. It will always survive and will try to thrive but once you bring in the chemical, pesticide and antibiotic foods into the equation your body is going to run into trouble. "What You Leave Out" is what enables your body the God-given remedial healing capabilities to engage. Then eating food in its highest biological form (organic plant-based foods) will nourish your body. This will give you all the amino acids, vitamins, minerals, glucose and essential fats you need to be satisfied and complete.

Just to clarify that when I'm talking about amino acids and proteins I am not specifically talking about animal proteins. I am stating this because of the protein addiction in our society and other industrial nations. Let me make it clear, you don't need animal protein to get enough amino acids/protein to live a healthy plant-based lifestyle. Although, you can have a minimal amount if desired but thinking that you absolutely need animal protein is just abstract science and not valid. Of course there are double blind studies that show that animal protein is essential but that's the reason I don't believe in double blind studies. They're not showing me enough variables so that alone exposes the weakness of the animal protein theory. We have to keep in mind that the body has around 100 trillion cells that interact with trillions of variables that make up the body's composition as a biological individual. This is indicative in reality when a person is focused on the outcome of their body which is totally different then a double blind study.

It is our responsibility to educate ourselves and be able

to tell the differences from all the promotional hype and people with an agenda for capital gains only. We have to be realistic, there are people that just want to take advantage of you, consciously or unconsciously, whether it's good or not. So please be aware!

"Many Lifestyle Factors"

Of course, there are many important factors with staying happy and preventing diseases that go into making a healthy lifestyle change besides "What You Leave Out and what we eat and drink. Remember, Your Healthy Journey is about a lifestyle change for a lifetime where you become spiritually grounded and emotionally and psychologically sound.

The thoughts we entertain on a regular basis are what controls how we live our life. If we dwell on them they will become a reality. I believe that your spiritual beliefs have a lot to do with your genetic expression. This is becoming a proven fact in cellular biology. I have seen this over the last 50 years of my practice but now the research and genetic scientists are catching up to this truth. Numerous people have told me that their condition runs in their family, their uncle, grandfather, mother or cousin and they think they can't get better. Many times, they are the easiest to help. It's mainly the epigenetic switches that are turned on or off by how you live your own lifestyle and what's passed down through your family's generational lifestyle that influences your health and longevity. So be very careful what you accept as facts. Thirty years ago, the things that were considered facts were nothing but misconceptions or evaluations of a process that was really abstract rather than real.

Let's get real, be practical and make a commitment to Your Healthy Journey!

Faith empowers you
Struggle makes you strong
Tragedy could give you wisdom
Humility comes with wisdom
Complaining makes you bitter
Love can be contagious
Only God is more important than
health

Fred Bisci